THREE AMERICAN
ARCHITECTS

THREE AMERICAN ARCHITECTS

RICHARDSON,

SULLIVAN, AND

WRIGHT, 1865–1915

JAMES F. O'GORMAN

THE UNIVERSITY OF CHICAGO PRESS
CHICAGO AND LONDON

JAMES F. O'GORMAN is the Grace Slack McNeil Professor of the History of American Art at Wellesley College. His other books include *H. H. Richardson: Architectural Forms for an American Society,* also published by the University of Chicago Press.

Illustrations on p. i: H. H. Richardson (top) Louis Henry Sullivan (center), Frank Lloyd Wright (bottom); on p. iii: Richardson's initials from the Allegheny County Courthouse (top), Sullivan's initials from the Schlesinger & Mayer Store (center), Wright's initials from Taliesin (bottom)

The University of Chicago Press, Chicago 60637
The University of Chicago Press, Ltd., London
© 1991 by The University of Chicago
All rights reserved. Published 1991
Printed in the United States of America

00 99 98 97 96 95 94 93 92   5 4 3 2

Library of Congress Cataloging-in-Publication Data

O'Gorman, James F.
    Three American architects : Richardson, Sullivan, and Wright,
1865–1915 / James F. O'Gorman.
        p.   cm.
    Includes bibliographical references.
    ISBN 0-226-62071-9
    1. Architecture, Modern—19th century—United States.
2. Architecture, Modern—20th century—United States.
3. Architecture—United States.   4. Richardson, H. H. (Henry
Hobson), 1838–1886—Criticism and interpretation.   5. Sullivan,
Louis H., 1856–1924—Criticism and interpretation.   6. Wright, Frank
Lloyd, 1867–1959—Criticism and interpretation.   I. Title.
NA710.035   1991   90-10957
720'.973'09034—dc20   CIP

To the Muses of Addison Street
Susan, Abigail, and Catalina

CONTENTS

ILLUSTRATIONS

America brings builders, and brings its own styles

Leaves of Grass

PREFACE

This essay describes the evolution of the forms created during three sequential American architectural careers: one that began in the 1860s and reached maturity about 1880, one that began in the 1870s and reached maturity about 1890, and one that began in the 1880s and reached maturity about 1900. This is a discussion of individual and collective achievement by the recognized trinity of American architecture: Henry Hobson Richardson (1838–86), Louis Henry Sullivan (1856–1924), and Frank Lloyd Wright (1867–1959). This work emphasizes the interrelationships among these three and focuses on their designs and executed buildings, which—we need to remind ourselves—are the primary records of achievement in architecture. Where I lean upon the support of the written word, I use, as much as possible, writings that stem from the period under review, the half century between the beginning of Richardson's professional career and the end of Wright's early years of production. Where I rely upon later writings, especially the revisionist polemics of Sullivan, Wright, and their apologists, I do so with expressed skepticism and only because no contemporary witness is available.

Architectural historians will recognize that this essay builds upon my earlier writings, especially my study of Frank Furness of 1973 and my book on Richardson of 1987 (although the close reader of the latter will find that I here extend and in some cases modify what I wrote there). Those historians will also be aware that the relationship among these three architects has been recognized at least since the publication of Lewis Mumford's *Brown Decades* in 1931. In chapter 3, "Towards Modern Architecture," Mumford wrote that "on Richardson's solid foundations, he [Sullivan] laid the cornerstone of the new organic architecture. Sullivan was the link between two greater masters, Richardson and Frank Lloyd Wright; and with the development of Wright's architecture . . . modern architecture in America was born." He also wrote that "the work of Richardson, Sullivan, and Wright, has been a conscious orientation of architecture toward new forms of expression." The reader will find that I largely agree with these conclusions, although a direct connection between the work of Richardson, Sullivan, and Wright and current practice—a connection crucial to the historians and apologists of the early 1930s—is no longer an issue. In my discussion of Richardson I emphasize his reinterpretation of the past; in my discussion of Wright I emphasize his continuity with the nineteenth century in general and Richardson in particular: how he built upon the past rather than heralded the future. In neither case is this understanding the whole story, although I think it fundamental. Like Mumford, I see Sullivan as a "link" between the other two. The work of these men is no less of interest for being firmly fixed in the history rather than the practice of architecture, and I explicitly reject any interpretation of this book as suggesting that these three men were precursors of International modernism or the olio of the present. (That may or may not be the case, but I neither state nor imply an opinion here.) But Mumford's study is too general and now too dated for the readership I address, and I have attempted to tell the story in sharper focus and greater richness of detail.

My subject is limited to the cumulative formal achievement of these piggy-backed careers. While I applaud the trend toward more inclusive methods of writing architectural history, to sharpen the focus of this work I have restricted myself to a discussion of the continuous evolution of the forms with which these architects solved the requirements of given building programs. I find it necessary to emphasize that my subject is limited to what these men built, not to what we might wish they had built: Richardson created no triple-deckers for Roxbury; Sullivan, no low-rent high-risers for Chicago; Wright, no public housing for any locale. My method is largely descriptive, and fixed upon representative works. Once these architects had evolved and explored a characteristic set of forms, which each of them did by his mid-forties, I cease my observations. My discussion of Richardson's work ends with his premature death in 1886, and my discussion of Sullivan's with the beginning of what I see as his decline during work on the Schlesinger & Mayer Store of 1898 to 1904. Although Wright was to enjoy an astonishingly vital career beyond his middle years, by the second decade of this century he had not only created a domestic architecture of his own but explored many of its possibilities. While discussions of Wright's early career usually break off somewhere around 1910, I see his rural retreat at Taliesin (built and rebuilt between 1911 and 1915) as the culminating domestic realization of the process described here.

I have also established a context within which each of these three careers

evolved. That context is both internal (that is, characterized by the historical relationships among the three) and external. While the relationships
among their representative works are my main focus, I have set them
against a generalized external backdrop. By the 1880s American society had
begun to achieve that split personality, that division into commercial centers
and domestic suburbs, toward which it had tended since early in the century
and that would mark it for the coming century at least. While the American
landscape then supported other zones, such as agricultural and industrial, it
is this backdrop of city and suburb that will be the focus of our attention
here. This is the framework for the maturation of those two especially
American building types: the tall office building towering above the mercantile core, and the detached, single-family dwelling nestled in its leafy
outskirts. This is the framework for the sexual separation in the middle and
upper-middle classes: the establishment of distinct spheres for men, who
ran the commercial world from downtown skyscrapers, and women, who
raised the next generation in domestic retreats, that George Santayana,
among others, recognized in "The Genteel Tradition in American Philosophy" as early as 1911 and that has only recently begun to blur. This is the
framework for literary works such as the Chicago novels of Henry Blake
Fuller, whose *Cliff-Dwellers* of 1893 is set within a multistoried commercial
block and whose *With the Procession* of 1895 treats of the domestic expec-
tations of the suburban middle class. And it is a particularly useful backdrop against which to describe the individual and collective architectural
achievements of Richardson, Sullivan, and Wright.

True, an underlying current in the following chapters will be a shared
Emersonian individualism. The stamp of self-reliance and ego-driven ambition emerges with increasing clarity over the course of these careers. Perhaps the most common element in the makeup of each of the trio was his
desire to shape a personal as well as an American architecture (in fact they
viewed the two as congruent) out of the collective materials available to him
at the start of his career. That they succeeded is implied when we speak of
a "Richardson" library, a "Sullivan" office building, a "Wright" house,
and thereby recognize that they were created as much for the architect to
satisfy his own professional or aesthetic ends as to satisfy a larger social
need. Richardson's libraries were abhorred by the American Library Association; Sullivan's many unbuilt projects bespeak a lack of satisfaction
among many of his clients. And in an oft-repeated statement that could well
be more generally applied, the *Architectural Record* in October 1911 said
that the design of Wright's Coonley House "is more advantageous to the

architect . . . than it is to the owner." Each of these men "signed" buildings with a personal monogram (see title page), literally put his own mark on his client's property, just as the contemporary painting was only a finished personal statement once the artist affixed his or her signature.

Sullivan and Wright defined themselves as nonconformists, outside of their profession, and as critics, set apart from their society; and in varying degrees these architects also sought design referents outside of society, as David Andrew has emphasized in his study of Sullivan. This alienation increasingly led them to turn for formal inspiration to nature, to the geological or biological analogy, leaving society to fend for itself. While their alienation may account in part for their achievement and their historical prominence, and it is the common chain linking their collective careers, it may also account for the demise of their influence, for the individualism of the late nineteenth century lost favor with the emergence of corporate America in the years before World War I.

Nonetheless, while individualism marks the biography of each of these men, taken together their careers form a coherent episode. I subscribe here to Barbara Tuchman's definition, near the end of the preface to her *Practicing History* (1981), of "human conduct as a steady stream running through endless fields of changing circumstances." The process through the following chapters will be cumulative, with each subsequent career dependent in part upon the previous one and in part upon new historical forces. And the work of each architect will perforce be described against the bifurcated society of the country. One of Richardson's principal historical achievements (in addition to the role of the Emersonian self-reliant architect he assumed in the eyes of his followers) was to provide patterns, however incomplete, for building types in two of the social zones that emerged in the aftermath of the Civil War: the urban commercial block and the suburban single-family house. In works such as the Marshall Field Wholesale Store and the Ames Gate Lodge and Potter House, he suggested a way to naturalize the profusion of imported stylistic possibilities dominant during the early careers of Sullivan and Wright. Accidents of history and biography made each of these types of prime importance to each of his followers: Sullivan (with his partner, Dankmar Adler) melding the Richardsonian solid with new structural materials and techniques and an ornamental richness conventionalized from nature to create blocky, variously articulated commercial buildings from the Wainwright to the Schlesinger & Mayer; and Wright appropriating Richardsonian quietude, new technology, Sullivanesque naturalism, and a century of residential planning and environmental theory to sprawling domestic retreats such as the Willits, Dana, Roberts, Robie, and Little houses. The work of the latter two architects, while not totally dependent upon the first, is unthinkable without Richardson's example. While each man evolved his own style, the work of the trinity forms a collective achievement.

While it is possible to write of a collective achievement in the work of Richardson, Sullivan, and Wright, it is necessary also to recognize the various levels of accomplishment in the work of each. Richardson's achievement remained incomplete; he died in midcareer. Sullivan's achievement remained flawed; he never developed a coherent statement, the "true normal type" (as he called it in 1896), of the tall commercial structure either in words or in buildings. Wright alone accomplished a complete and consistent expression of his aims, especially in residential design; and that is one reason his reputation among both professionals and public rises well above that of either predecessor. Although he would never admit it, he needed the work of those predecessors to achieve that eminence.

There are now, in general as well as specialized libraries, shelves groaning under the weight of multiple tomes devoted to the accomplishments of these three men, and with alarming acceleration more books appear every year (including my own), although there has been no one work (other than a general account such as Mumford's chapter) that concentrates upon the trio as a collective phenomenon. This discussion is selective rather than comprehensive. Because information about the individual architects is readily available elsewhere, it does not seem necessary here to mention more than briefly the sources of inspiration other than those relating to my central theme, nor to discuss works by each of these architects other than those that illuminate my thesis, to reiterate their personal or professional biographies or those of their clients except as it furthers my discussion, to recapitulate all the conflicting scholarly arguments currently in vogue, or to footnote every publication consulted. Brevity is high on my list of intentions. My aim is to discuss only those aspects of these three careers during the years covered that apply to the theme of transformation, of continuously interlocking achievement, of continuity and change. My aim is to take a bird's-eye view of my subject and report what I see. That I fly on wings partially feathered by others is obvious, and to the extent possible within my self-imposed limits, they are recognized in the text, selected reading, or following acknowledgments.

There is no way I can acknowledge all the many teachers, colleagues, students, friends, and critics who have over the years enriched my understanding of this subject. For recent contributions, conversations, contrary opinions, and/or contacts, I want to thank Richard Betts, Robert Twombly, Paul Sprague, George Thomas, Robert Brown, David Brownlee, Randell Makinson, Allen Brooks, Carolyn Pitts, William Pierson, Marshall Erdman, Charles Montooth, Anthony Puttnam, and Michael Lewis. John O. Holzhueter called my attention to the letter from Wright to Cudworth Beye in the Beye Collection in the Archives of the State Historical Society of Wisconsin. Susan Danly, Cervin Robinson, Robert Kline, Peter Fergusson, and Jack Quinan read the manuscript during its development and suggested various points of improvement. I especially want to thank both Elaine Harrington and Kevin Harrington for their perusal of an advanced draft; they made many improvements, and it is not their fault that I did not always follow their wise suggestions. Carol Bolton Betts brought her editorial skills to an even more advanced draft, for which the reader is in her debt. The National Endowment for the Humanities awarded me a fellowship, and Wellesley College granted me leave to write the text during the past winter.

J. F. O'G.

Philadelphia
31 May 1989

INTRODUCTION:
MUSE, MASTER, AND MAN

Let us go back exactly a century, to the sixteenth floor of that blunt tower rising above the Auditorium Building on the north side of the Congress Parkway between Michigan and Wabash avenues in Chicago, a structure that now houses Roosevelt University (see fig. 55). In 1890 the architectural firm of Adler and Sullivan was newly installed in this aerie above the massive stone block that formed its first major accomplishment. The commission officially became the firm's late in December 1886. The building, combining offices, hotel, and opera house, was dedicated in December 1889 with the help of President Benjamin Harrison and the diva Adelina Patti. The Auditorium's completion capped the resurgence of Chicago after the devastating fire of nearly two decades earlier, and it marked the arrival of a major new presence in the architectural history of the United States.

The firm consisted of an older member, its business partner and engineering specialist, Dankmar Adler, and a younger designer, Louis H. Sullivan. Each of these was in turn assisted by a secondary figure: Paul Mueller, perhaps best described as a construction supervisor, reinforced Adler's role; Frank Lloyd Wright backed up Sullivan. A large force of draftsmen made up the rest of the personnel. The layout of the office, published in *Engineering & Building Record* for June 1890, formed a perfect diagram of the organization: Adler's office was accessible from the reception area, as was Mueller's, which also connected to the pool of perhaps thirty draftsmen through a glazed partition. Sullivan's retreat nestled across the consultation room from Adler's, in the southeast corner of the tower, with Wright's office adjacent to it and also divided from the drafting force by a glass wall.

Adler and Sullivan's move from the old Borden Block, an office building of 1880 that was one of the earliest results of their collaboration, marked the partnership's arrival among the foremost architectural firms in the city, and it heralded the beginning of a number of urban commercial works upon which the corporate fame of the firm and the individual fame of Louis Sullivan principally rest. These include the Wainwright Building in St. Louis

(1890–91; fig. 61), the Union Trust Building in St. Louis (1892–93; fig. 65), the Chicago Stock Exchange Building (1893), and the Guaranty (later Prudential) Building in Buffalo (1894–95; fig. 63). Corporate tranquility and accomplishment were short-lived, however, for Wright left in 1893, and in 1895 the partnership itself ended, with each of the principals pursuing an independent career. For a while Sullivan held onto the lofty office and continued to add to the list of important commercial works with the Bayard (later Condict) Building in New York City (1897–98; fig. 66) and the Schlesinger & Mayer Store (later Carson Pirie Scott) in Chicago (1898–1904; fig. 67), but from the turn of the century his career was clearly on the wane. The years until his death in 1924 saw a decline in the number of commissions he erected, a number which included a series of small-town banks of great charm if arguably less significance than his urban commercial work (fig. 71). It was the achievement of that brief period in the 1890s, however, that is the focus of our interest here.

Adler's contribution to that achievement, and through him Paul Mueller's, ought not be denied, and of late their contribution has begun to receive its historical due. Two other connections capture our attention, however: one with Wright, the helper at Sullivan's side; the other with the work of H. H. Richardson, who had died just before the commission for the Auditorium materialized but whose recently finished Marshall Field Wholesale Store in Chicago had had a major impact upon it. The confluence of these three creative personalities—of Richardson, Sullivan, and Wright—representing in 1890 the past, the present, and the future of a paramount interlude in late nineteenth-century American architecture, forms the subject of the following chapters.

Wright had joined the partners in the Borden Block early in 1888. He arrived as a young draftsman with some experience in the Chicago office of Joseph L. Silsbee, an Eastern-born architect and gifted designer of domestic buildings in the picturesque, shingled mode currently fashionable in the suburbs and on the seacoast from Maine to Maryland. Wright was taken on with other assistants to help prepare the drawings for the Auditorium, a commission of greater importance than anything the firm had heretofore undertaken. And there are indeed surviving studies for Auditorium ornament that are attributed to Wright's hand.

By the time of the move to the Auditorium tower, the young draftsman had become Sullivan's chief assistant. Writing about this period some half century later, in his brief and woolly accounts of the days and nights spent in Sullivan's employ, Wright refers to himself as the "pencil" in "lieber

Meister's" hand. In his *Autobiography* (1932, revised 1943), and more tellingly in his *Genius and the Mobocracy* (1949), Wright alludes to the period spent behind the "wide windows overlooking the vast lighted city lying peacefully by the lake." Wright suggests a closeness between master and "pencil" that borders on a confusion of identities. One result is that the reader can easily assume that Wright did much of the design-drafting for some of the works celebrated as Sullivan's finest. Another impression Wright seeks to convey is that Sullivan, and by extension Wright, too, had little use for the work of their fellow architects. He fleetingly mentions late-night sessions between master and man, with the master doing all the talking, not, as one might suppose, about the state of their profession or the work of their contemporaries. Sullivan's oratorical focus was upon the greats of literature, philosophy, and music whom he "venerated": Whitman, Spencer, and Wagner, in particular. Yet Wright cannot help mentioning other names that surely came up during these sessions, the names of architects whom Sullivan also admired. There were his partner, Adler; the friend of his early Chicago days, John Edelmann; and John Root, the promising Chicago associate of Daniel Burnham who died so young in 1891. H. H. Richardson, too, must have concerned the two in their lofty, late-night perch, although Wright with characteristic dissemblance makes it sound as if Richardson's name went unspoken at this time, that he learned only later of Sullivan's lamentable admiration for his predecessor: "But later I discovered his secret respect, leaning a little toward envy (I was ashamed to suspect), for H. H. Richardson. Just the same and nevertheless he liked and trusted *me*" (Wright's emphasis). Wright's jealousy, still so strongly expressed after so many years, rings clear in these revealing sentences and suggests the mistrust underlying his lifetime reluctance to credit Richardson with any impact on his master's or his own work.

The period in which Wright joined Sullivan, the late 1880s, marked the apogee in American architecture of "picturesque eclecticism," a term used to denote both the dependence of most architects on the bewildering variety of forms available from the history of building both classical and nonclassical, both Eastern and Western, and their characteristic design of buildings of dramatic, asymmetrical silhouette and sophisticated, accretive detail (fig. 4). The result was the riot of shrill creations once popularly labeled "Victorian horrors." At one level of understanding, Richardson's work was characterized by his revival of French and Spanish Romanesque architectural forms (fig. 13). Like his contemporaries, he was an eclectic architect, but his work stood apart from theirs because he chose sources distinct from

3

their classical, Gothic, or Islamic quotations. At another and more profound level, Richardson disciplined the picturesque aspects of contemporary design, including the quotations of historical detail, in favor of a return to architectural fundamentals: solid wall, arched void, roof, mass, light and shadow, natural materials, usually ashlar stone (fig. 23). Unlike the sophisticated pastiches of his contemporaries, his works were "primitive" in the sense that they were basic, elemental, forceful interpretations of building programs and historical forms. This too set him apart from his peers.

At the end of his all-too-brief career, in the mid-1880s, Richardson designed for Chicago two works of seminal importance in the development of Sullivan and Wright: the Marshall Field Wholesale Store (fig. 26) on Adams Street between Franklin and Fifth (now Wells), a few blocks west of the Auditorium, and the John J. Glessner House (fig. 34) on Prairie Avenue south of the Loop. (A third building, an 1885 house for Franklin MacVeagh, seems to have made less of an impact.) These works certainly provided immediate inspiration in the evolving careers of Sullivan and his assistant.

We have only Wright's belated and highly colored notes about the interaction between Sullivan and him in their Auditorium loft high above the metropolis by the lake. Wright suggests that the master held him a captive audience for his thoughts until he had to make a dash for the last commuter train to his suburban home. The exact content of those soliloquies is of course lost, but the scenario of teacher and student is one Sullivan himself recreated for his "Kindergarten Chats," a series of papers originally published in *Interstate Architect and Builder* between February 1901 and February 1902. Just as Wright noted in his *Autobiography* that Sullivan needed to think out loud even to the point of forgetting Wright's presence, so the narrator of the "Chats" at one point remarks, "I thought aloud. You happened to be present." Surely the "Chats" preserve something of the essence of those late-night monologues at the top of the town.

As Wright observed, Sullivan had only contempt for the works of his contemporaries, and the "Chats" begin by bashing a number of recent picturesque or eclectic Chicago buildings. Number VI, however, containing the quote about the narrator's oblivion to the presence of his pupil, is devoted to the Marshall Field Wholesale Store. "Let us pause, my son, at this oasis in our desert," begins the master, and during this interruption in the stream of vitriol, Sullivan will pen some of the most moving praises ever directed by one American architect toward the commercial masterpiece of another. Among the paeans of "The Oasis," one in particular bears repetition here: "Buildings such as this, and there are not many of them, stand as land-

4

marks, as promontories, to the navigator. They show when and where architecture has taken on its outburst of form as a grand passion—amid a
host of stage-struck-wobbling mockeries." So Sullivan saw Richardson's
Marshall Field store when he wrote the "Chats," and so he must have valued
it when he held Wright captive hour after late-night hour in the Auditorium tower, for so he saw it when he was designing the Auditorium itself a
few years earlier. Sullivan penetrated the Renaissance-Romanesque references of the Field store to grasp its essential character as a quiet and massive
foil to the shrill histrionics of contemporary work.

The story of Sullivan's reaction to the emerging Field store has been told
many times. The commission for the older building came into Richardson's
office in Brookline, Massachusetts, in April 1885; construction began in the
fall of the same year, and the building was opened in June 1887, more than
a year after Richardson's death in April 1886. It was a blockbuster of a
building: a simple rectangular solid of reddish Massachusetts sandstone and
Missouri granite, the principal facades of which were of seven stories organized by layers of arcuated openings embracing groups of floors except at
the top, where trabeated voids heralded the horizontal cornice. To Sullivan
in the "Chats" it was "four-square and brown, . . . a monument to trade,
to the organized commercial spirit, to the power and progress of the age."
And as we have seen, he also said it was a landmark for the architectural
navigator.

Richardson's spirit was particularly evident around the Adler and Sullivan office during the late 1880s and early 1890s, and it suffused the very
building it occupied after 1890, for the Auditorium directly reflected the
impact of the Field facades upon Sullivan's development. Sullivan began
designing the exterior of the Auditorium late in 1886, before Wright arrived on the scene, and was to spend vast sums of energy and money revis-
ing the project over the next months. Two early schemes, preserved in photographs of lost drawings, were picturesque Romanesque in design. They
were superficially Richardsonian in their use of half-circular arches but they
were given (1) polychromatic treatment in "brick and efflorescent terra
cotta," as Wright later remembered, (2) agglutinate character by the addition of oriels, bays, and other features of the currently fashionable Queen
Anne style, and (3) a picturesque silhouette enriched by pointed terminals
crowned by a high peaked roof over the tower. By early 1887 the Field store
was nearing completion, and Sullivan must have realized that the picturesque aspects were just what Richardson's finest commercial structure had
eliminated. He chopped his Auditorium tower off square and scoured his

facades, eventually elongating Richardson's elevational scheme in adapting it to a block several stories higher. Wright arrived in time to help with the decoration of the interior. It was the first of many decidedly Richardsonian works to issue from the office of Adler and Sullivan.

The Walker Warehouse in Chicago of 1887–89, an arcuated smooth stone block that is no longer standing, was among the first and finest of these. According to Wright's characteristically denigrating account in *Genius and the Mobocracy*, "The master brought the manila stretch [sic] with the elevation penciled upon it, [and] laid it over my [drafting]board with the remark, 'Wright, there is the last word in the Romanesque.' I puzzled over that remark a lot. What business had he with the Romanesque?" Again, Wright dissembled. His published attitude toward Richardson (whose name in this era was synonymous with Romanesque) vacillated over the course of his long life, but as we shall see, in 1888, at the moment of which he later wrote, he was himself engaged in a close scrutiny of the Glessner House, tentatively adapting many of its features for a series of three houses commissioned of the firm by Victor Falkenau (fig. 74). It was merely the first of Wright's long series of Richardsonian transformations.

At this moment too, Sullivan's and Wright's knowledge of Richardson and his reductive Romanesque was derived not only from the rising bulks of the Field store and the Glessner and MacVeagh houses but from several publications Sullivan had in his library. He owned portfolios of photographs of Richardson's Austin Hall at Harvard and his buildings for the Ames family in North Easton, Massachusetts (fig. 24), publications described by Cervin Robinson in *Architecture Transformed* as providing "a first systematic view in published photographs of contemporary architecture." More important, he had the memorial volume dedicated to the older architect written by Mariana Griswold Van Rensselaer, a leading Eastern critic of art and architecture. *Henry Hobson Richardson and His Works*, a large, handsome, and well-illustrated folio, appeared in May 1888. With the availability of Richardson's local buildings and these books, both master and pencil were more than adequately provided with visual guideposts for their course through that "host of stage-struck-wobbling mockeries." Moreover, with the exception of a little-known 1865 memoir by William Wheildon of Solomon Willard (the designer of Boston's Bunker Hill Monument and other neoclassical designs) and an even more obscure "brief memoir" of Providence's Thomas Tefft by Edwin M. Stone (1869), which were slight works compared to Van Rensselaer's beautifully wrought, hefty tome bearing an epigraph from Emerson's "Art" on its title page, her memorial was the first full-blown monograph dedicated to an American architect. Willard and Tefft had been architects of largely local significance; Van Rensselaer presented Richardson's career as supraregional. Sullivan and Wright were both psychologically disposed to envy that tribute to individual genius and national reputation. (It might be suggested that both wrote autobiographies during lean periods of later life, when it looked as if no biographer might ever turn to them.)

So, when the firm of Adler and Sullivan moved into the sixteenth-floor suite high above its new Richardsonian block, with Wright carried along as Sullivan's assistant, three major creative personalities came together in spirit if not in fact. Here were muse, master, and man. Richardson was the provider of inspirational landmarks pointing the way through dangerous contemporary architectural waters to the safety of disciplined and personal achievement; Sullivan was the guiding designer of the firm; and Wright was the pencil in his hand. It is of the cumulative accomplishments of this trinity of independent, interdependent architects that the following essay treats. This is the story of Richardson's pioneering, unperfected achievements in the creation of formal prototypes for both urban commercial architecture and suburban residential design, and the impact of his achievements on his two distinguished followers. It is further the story of Sullivan's use of Richardsonian inspiration combined with the elements of his own history: his brief work for Philadelphia's Frank Furness and the influence, through Furness, of English and French theories of conventionalized ornamental design, as well as the latest technology in the creation of the tall urban office building "artistically considered." And it is the story of Wright's beginnings with Sullivan during Sullivan's early and most intensely Richardsonian phase, of his own contributions to this narration of continuity and change: of his Jeffersonian inclinations, of his adaptation of nineteenth-century domestic planning and theories of conventional ornament to ideals of form and structure, and of his embrace of the machine and its structural potential—all in the evolution of the suburban or rural prairie house. These three successive careers mark three successive phases of a search for an architecture distinguishable from its European roots, an architecture reflective of America's nineteenth-century separation into commercial downtowns and residential suburbs, an architecture that would comply with the longstanding demands of Emerson, Whitman, and others that America generate cultural forms of its own. It is also the story of three different searches for an individual distinction within the evolution of an architecture to fill that prescription.

7

1 Henry Hobson Richardson (1838–86) in 1879 (courtesy of the Society for the Preservation of New England Antiquities, Codman Family Manuscripts Collection)

1

DISCIPLINING THE PICTURESQUE

When H. H. Richardson (fig. 1) stepped off the transatlantic liner at New York in October 1865, he had just turned twenty-seven years old, had just ended an educational exile in Paris begun before the outbreak of the Civil War, and had decided to begin his career in architecture, not in his native New Orleans nor in his adopted Boston but in New York City, the metropolis fast becoming the financial and cultural capital of the United States. (He was eventually to set up permanent shop in Brookline, a suburb of Boston.) With his disembarkation he joined the few academically trained architects in the country, and he could expect to assume quickly an important place in his chosen profession. Although he was "prepared for a hard time for some months," as he wrote his brother in an unpublished letter now at Harvard University, he had "confidence in ultimate success." However high his confidence, however exalted his youthful aspirations, he could not possibly have imagined the historical dimensions of that "ultimate success." Richardson carried with him off that ocean liner a vague desire to create a "bold, rich, living architecture" that was to have, as it came near realization during the next two decades, a varied and profound impact on the course of American building.

Born in Louisiana in 1838 and educated at Harvard College during the second half of the 1850s, Richardson had trained for his career at the Ecole des Beaux-Arts in Paris in the atelier of Jules André and in the office of Théodore Labrouste. From his youth in the South he brought a knowledge of the compact, hip-roofed classical architecture of the antebellum era; and in Cambridge and Boston he must have noticed the austere granite architecture of midcentury. In Paris he followed Richard Morris Hunt, who had studied and worked there in the 1840s and 1850s, as an *élève* of French theory and practice of architecture, an experience matched by no other American-born architect at the time of his return from abroad. Any well-rounded assessment of Richardson's achievement must include an understanding of the profound impact of his experience in Paris as well as of the

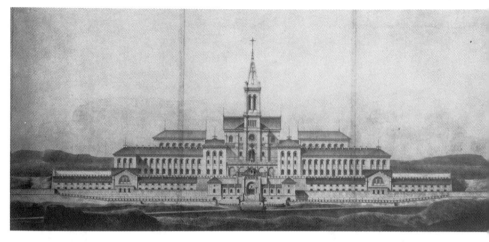

2 Julien Guadet, project for a hospice in the Alps, 1864, elevation (from Arthur Drexler, ed., *Architecture of the Ecole des Beaux-Arts*, 1977)

way he absorbed that experience into his own programmatic mission.

Classicism had been the French national style since the time of Francis I. By the nineteenth century, that classicism had been developed and codified in the ateliers of the Ecole into a system of education of such strength that it could withstand attempted inroads by Gothic revivalists such as E. E. Viollet-le-Duc during Richardson's tenure in Paris. As a new student Richardson drew from casts of antique statuary and copied from the graphic works of Piranesi, the eighteenth-century Roman whose imaginative views of ancient architecture raised classical style to a new monumentality. But the French method went beyond the classical orders. As Richardson's friend Julien Guadet later wrote, the Ecole taught the science of design, not a style. Instruction centered around a method that included both rational spatial organization and a sequential planning process based on the classical armature of balanced hierarchical axes. The ordinal overlay was optional. During Richardson's stay in Paris, in 1864, Guadet won the coveted Prix de Rome with a project for an astylar Romanesque mountaintop monastery whose round-arched forms pyramid toward the apex of a central church tower (fig. 2). It was an image Richardson carried with him into maturity.

The Ecole planning process organized the elements of a building program into two fundamental spatial types: primary, or those embodying the raison d'être of the building, and secondary, or those making the primary spaces usable. The architect Louis Kahn was much later to call these "served" and "servant" spaces. In a school, for example, a primary or served space would be a classroom; a secondary or servant space would be a

10

corridor, a stairway, or a lavatory. The clear analysis of the building program into served and servant spaces followed by the equally clear synthesis of these parts into a balanced hierarchical axial arrangement in both plan and elevation was the essence of Ecole design. The system was, of course, self-justifying: the best result was a building that clearly articulated its program according to Ecole principles.

The student arrived at his solution by a process beginning with an *esquisse,* or quick sketch, in which he worked out the essentials of a problem graphically during a short period of isolation. Subsequent development of the design had to follow closely the *parti* established *en loge.* He thus developed the ability to reduce nimbly the complexity of a building program to its constituent served and servant spaces and arrange them axially into a clearly balanced hierarchy. Richardson learned how to generate quickly a central idea from which all subsequent development flowed. Among the scant remains of his student days is an *esquisse* for a casino over a thermal mineral spring, an Ecole project of June 1863 (fig. 3). In his thumbnail plan

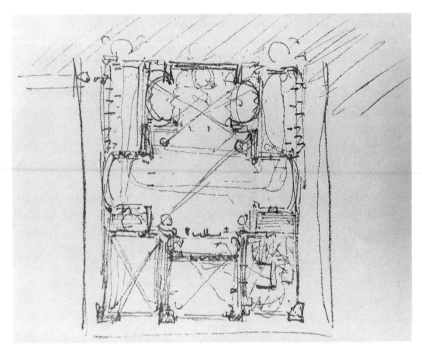

3 H. H. Richardson, project for a casino, 1863, sketch plan (from Van Rensselaer, *Richardson,* 1888)

Richardson gathered the various prescribed elements of the task into a simple geometric shape: a cruciform space slightly elongated in one direction within a circumscribing rectangle. Through the imposition of balanced hierarchial axes, the linear sequence of verbally specified discrete spaces was transformed into an interdependent geometric system expressed in a simple graphic shape comprehensible at a glance. It was another image the architect would recreate time and time again. We can judge from his mature works, in which he eschewed classical details, that knowledge of the *esquisse* process and the rational analysis of building program far outweighed the trappings of classical style in the aspiring architect's homeward baggage.

Richardson was twenty when he journeyed through England to France in the spring of 1859 to begin his European training. He knew contemporary English work, but in the more than six impressionable years he had spent studying and working within the Parisian milieu, he must have become thoroughly Gallic and indeed, although he wore clothes of English make, was said to prefer to speak French in the early days after his return to this country. With such training he might have vied with Richard Hunt to become the leading Francophile architect in the United States, and in fact he later admitted to his first biographer that "it would not cost me a bit of trouble to build French buildings from . . . [Boston] to Philadelphia." But he was quick to add that "that is not what I want to do." Richardson was cosmopolite more than Francophile. Although it is doubtful that he clearly recognized it as he left the New York docks for a Brooklyn roominghouse that October day in 1865, Richardson's ultimate aim was to merge French method and European architectural tradition with sources closer to home to create an architectural imagery for post–Civil War America distinct from that of his professional peers. What he wanted was to create a personal architectural imagery.

The architectural situation in this country when Richardson returned just after the Civil War revolved around a series of questions posed by practitioners and theorists alike: How are we to incorporate the new materials and techniques of the industrial age such as plate glass and structural metal? What in the modern world is the role of the professional architect and what, for that matter, is a "professional architect"? How are we to plan and articulate the varieties of new buildings made necessary by a pluralistic society? How, in a progressive, sophisticated era, are the findings of historical scholarship to be incorporated into the process of design? In what style are we to build? For Richardson personally, however, the chief question seems to have been, How might I establish an individual and a national identity within the world of architectural design? It was the kind of question that, in broader cultural terms, also preoccupied Emerson and Whitman.

American designers and builders had always followed the lead of European fashion, first as shapers of the colonial outposts of England, Holland, France, Spain, and other Old World countries, and after independence, as provincial exponents of the successive classical- and medieval-inspired international styles. By the Civil War American architects were profitably aware of developments in three European national centers in particular: England, where the polychromatic picturesque Gothic-derived architecture popularly associated with the name of John Ruskin was the dominant mode from the late 1840s; France, where the academic classicism of the néo-Grec era and the Second Empire vied with Viollet-le-Duc's theories of metallic building based upon a rational analysis of Gothic structure; and Germany, where Renaissance- and Romanesque-inspired arcuated blocks carried the name *Rundbogenstil*. Immigrant architects as well as publications out of each of these countries provided American designers with knowledge of the latest in European theory and design.

In a century marked by stylistic revivals generated and fueled by art-historical scholarship as well as grand-tourism among clients, the proliferation of available prototypes led to visual profusion and confusion. Early in the century a spirit of historicism prevailed, so that an architect would usually, if designing a building from precedent, be content for prototype with one landmark or the style of one era or, at most, the parts of visually compatible landmarks or eras. So, William Strickland's Second Bank of the United States in Philadelphia (1818–24), a classical building composed of a Greek exterior with porticoes based on Stuart and Revett's reconstruction of the Parthenon and an interior with Roman vaults and Greek orders, is nonetheless visually coherent. So was Town and Davis's Tudor building of the 1830s for New York University, with its central chapel derived from some printed view of that at King's College, Cambridge. Arthur Gilman expressed the extreme position of the era. In Boston's *North American Review* for April 1844 he said of the revived Gothic alone that "an incongruous intermingling of the manner of one century with that of another, is a total violation of architectural propriety." By the post–Civil War era, however, the climate of opinion had changed. Eclecticism now prevailed, with its free selection from diverse and to our eyes often conflicting sources. Scholarship provided forms from as far afield as the Near and Far East, and architects thought that progressive theory demanded their use in what now seems a bewildering disarray. Thus, Henry Van Brunt could write in the introduction to his translation of Viollet-le-Duc's *Discourses* (1875), "where [data about] architectural monuments and traditions have accumulated to the vast extent they have . . . , the question is not whether we shall use them . . . , but how shall we choose among them." Even where conventional sources prevailed, that is to say, where architects stuck to the current work of England and France, eclecticism created a dramatic shift from the historicism of earlier in the century.

There were architects such as Frederick Withers and Calvert Vaux, English immigrants both, who in works such as New York's Jefferson Market Courthouse (1874–77) carried over to this country nearly unchanged the prevailing polychromatic picturesque Gothic of their London peers (fig. 4). This building is vertically proportioned with lean, asymmetrical tower, pointed openings in a variety of designs, and colorful, contrasting materials. Other architects such as Alfred B. Mullett, in works such as the Post Office building in St. Louis (1874–82), carried over to this country nearly unchanged the Second Empire, mansard-capped classicism of their Parisian counterparts (fig. 5). The Post Office was a measured, monochromatic block articulated by tiers of orders and focused in each facade by a central *pavillon*. The planar richness of Anglo-eclectic works is replaced here by a plastic play of light-and-shadow patterns that create parallel visual vibrations. And there were others, such as Frank Furness and some of his colleagues in and out of Philadelphia, who could work competently in either or other styles or could creatively combine them into an eclectic bouillabaisse.

Furness's work is a useful foil to that of Richardson. They were born thirteen-and-a-half months apart (Furness being the younger), and although he never realized his ambition to attend the Ecole, Furness did study in the late 1850s in the New York atelier of Richard Morris Hunt, himself newly returned from Paris. Both Richardson and Furness received their first commissions in 1866; both reached important professional thresholds with buildings erected in the early 1870s; and both went on to distinguished careers, with Richardson's cut short by his early death in the mid-1880s and Furness's reaching into the first years of the new century. Despite this chronological congruence, however, these men created dramatically different buildings (even where Furness's show the influence of Richardson), and each career bears a dramatically different relationship to the development of American architecture. The influence of each, however, was to be felt by Louis Sullivan, and through him, by Frank Lloyd Wright.

The 1860s saw the proliferation of French- and English-inspired design in the cities of the East and Midwest. The 1870s saw the proliferation of an

4 Frederick Withers and Calvert Vaux, Jefferson Market Courthouse, New York City, 1874–77, exterior (photo: author)

eclecticism derived from the merger of these and other historical sources. Eclecticism marked Furness's work especially. In 1871, in partnership with George W. Hewitt, Furness won the competition for the design of the Pennsylvania Academy of the Fine Arts at Broad and Cherry streets in Philadelphia, with a building blatantly mixing forms from a variety of sources (fig.

5 Alfred B. Mullet, Post Office Building, St. Louis, 1874–82, exterior (photo: author)

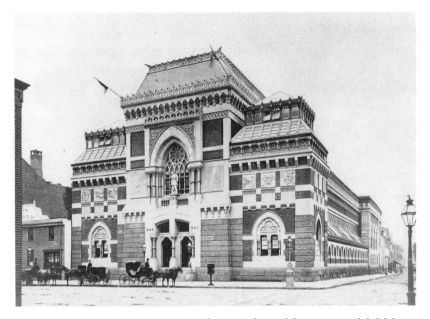

6 Frank Furness and George Hewitt, Pennsylvania Academy of the Fine Arts, Philadelphia, 1871–76, Broad Street front (photo: Frederick Gutekunst, courtesy of the Archives, Pennsylvania Academy of the Fine Arts, Philadelphia)

6). In particular the eastern facade on Broad Street is a textbook example of eclecticism, with, among other references, a symmetrical tripartite format lifted from a neoclassical work like John Haviland's nearby Pennsylvania Institution for the Deaf and Dumb (1824–26); a central, mansarded *pavillon* rising above flanking wings that repeats the organization of such Second Empire buildings as Boston's Old City Hall (1862–65) by Gridley J. F. Bryant and Arthur Gilman (but which ultimately stems from portions of the Louvre in Paris, the chef d'oeuvre of mid-nineteenth-century French classicism designed in the 1850s by Lefuel and Visconti assisted by Furness's mentor, Richard Morris Hunt); and polychromy and pointed arches that derive from the northern Italian Gothic by way of Ruskin's theoretical writings and the work of Victorian architects in London. (References to a variety of French and English sources, as we shall see, are also to be found in the ornamental details on this facade and throughout the interior.) The building lacks only the dynamic asymmetrical silhouette characteristic of picturesque eclecticism, and that Furness achieved in a variety of other works ranging from the Rodef Shalom Synagogue (1869–71) to the University of

17

Pennsylvania Library (1888–91). Furness was a major master of the multifarious, drawing bits and pieces from a variety of sources and combining them in his buildings into strident and gesticulating patchworks. And he was just one outstanding exponent of the picturesque, that visually rich architectural episode that colored the cities and towns of America, especially through the 1870s and 1880s—the years of Richardson's activity.

Richardson's first works reflected this situation. Having visited London and studied in Paris, he wore English clothes and spoke French. Possessed

7 Gambrill and Richardson, Grace Church, West Medford, Mass., 1867–69, exterior (photo: Jean Baer O'Gorman)

8 Gambrill and Richardson, William Dorsheimer House, Buffalo, 1868–71, exterior (photo: Margaret Henderson Floyd)

of a library of architectural reference works both English and French, he was well prepared to oscillate between the two sources as his early commissions warranted. The Harvard "old boy" network and his rare professional qualifications guaranteed that jobs would be forthcoming after some initial idle months, and he received his first commission just over a year after disembarkation. In such juvenilia (designed nominally in partnership with Charles D. Gambrill) as the Church of the Unity in Springfield, Massachusetts (1866–69), and Grace Church in West Medford, Massachusetts (1867–69), both of which are picturesque Gothic works, Richardson drew heavily upon English ecclesiastical sources (fig. 7). On the other hand, in his own house on Staten Island (1868–69) and the William Dorsheimer House in Buffalo (1868–71) he relied on his knowledge of French and, in the latter, néo-Grec domestic design (fig. 8). The plan he sketched about 1869 for a hospital in Worcester, Massachusetts, a large complex with sexually segregated wards flanking a shared, axially placed kitchen, chapel, and administration block, showed to what extent he had mastered French hierarchical planning. In the High School at Worcester, Massachusetts (1869–71), finally, he concocted an eclectic gaucherie combining balanced French planning with English polychromatic details and picturesque silhouette that must have awakened him to the fact that such design by accumulation was not for him, for he was soon to change course and sail off on a very different tack.

Richardson, to be sure, did not change direction overnight. His projected church for Columbus, Ohio, published late in 1872, is round-arched but otherwise polychromatic picturesque. His William Watts Sherman House of 1874–76 at Newport, a design exhibiting major contributions by the hand of his assistant, Stanford White, may be his most anglophilic work, as its living hall, rambling gabled forms, half-timbering, pargetting, and other embellishments drew heavily upon the current Queen Anne style of his English architectural peers Richard Norman Shaw and Eden Nesfield. As late as 1876 he created a masterpiece of picturesque asymmetry at the Winn Memorial Library at Woburn, Massachusetts (fig. 22), although by then he was otherwise working in a more disciplined direction. His project for the Connecticut State Capitol of 1871 or 1872, on the other hand, is an unadulterated exercise in Ecole-directed organization. It envisioned a cruciform plan containing entrance, Senate, House, and Supreme Court grouped around a central *salle des pas perdus* rising in three dimensions to the apex of the central tower. Gradually over the middle of the 1870s, however, overt reliance on contemporary English and French approaches gave way in Richardson's work to an appropriation of both more immediate and more remote sources.

The change is noticeable in two Boston ecclesiastical works of the early 1870s. The Brattle Square (1869–73) and Trinity (1872–77) churches each displays one of the sources with which he had begun to experiment: the *Rundbogenstil*—related Boston granite style and the Romanesque of the south of France and of Spain. This shift away from current English and French quotations immediately set Richardson apart from his contemporaries and sent him in a direction toward his mature and disciplined works of the decade's end.

The Brattle Square Church is an asymmetrical composition of smooth buff puddingstone and reddish sandstone, with openings created by semicircular arches of alternating voussoirs. Though of its time, it is also a hushed and harmonious statement compared to the contemporary Worcester High School; and while it might be called Romanesque, it would appear to reflect

Richardson's tentative turn to the simpler forms of the *Rundbogenstil* and the traditional stone architecture of the Boston vicinity. Round-arched cubical masonry design inspired by German work of the first half of the century had made an impact on this country, for example, in the secular buildings of Providence's Thomas Tefft and in some of the ecclesiastical works of Richard Upjohn. The latter's gray granite chapel at Bowdoin College in Brunswick, Maine (1844–55) comes easily to mind (fig. 9). The urban branch of this pattern of stone building emerges from the granite Greek Revival work of Alexander Parris and other local architects. By midcentury there was an identifiable "Boston granite style" of commercial building exemplified, for example, in the portside warehouses of G. J. F. Bryant and his various associates. In these foursquare buildings, the prismatic granite block formed the module of the design. Stacked into regular ashlar walls penetrated by regularly spaced rectangular voids and capped by rudimentary cornices, the granite unit generated a reductive, monumental, monochromatic architecture suited to the fundamentally economic function of the warehouse.

But this stringent, lithic style was not confined to commercial building alone. Boston midcentury architects adapted it to other purposes as well. The brothers Hammatt and Joseph Billings fronted their Boston Museum on Tremont Street (1845–46) with a granite palazzo facade punched through with regularly spaced, round-arched openings visible through a filigree of iron balconies (fig. 10). The German-born designer Paul Schulze created in Boylston Hall at Harvard (1857–58) an undecorated, rock-faced granite college building with round-headed openings that was clearly akin to the warehouses downtown. Since Schulze must also have known the *Rundbogenstil* at its source, Boylston Hall represents the marriage of these two related styles. And since H. H. Richardson as a Harvard undergraduate was just beginning to consider architecture as a career when Boylston opened, he must certainly have taken a keen interest in this rising example of the latest in building form. This round-arched stone architecture had a regularity, a rationale, that would have prepared Richardson for the design methods he encountered at the Ecole in Paris. And this round-arched stone architecture, whether it stemmed from the *Rundbogenstil* or grew out of the granite Greco-Roman work of early nineteenth-century Boston, was available as an alternate source upon which Richardson could draw when he had exhausted his patience with current French and English forms. Brattle Square was no triumph of design, but it did show that Richardson intended to move on to other expressions. His Hampden County Courthouse of

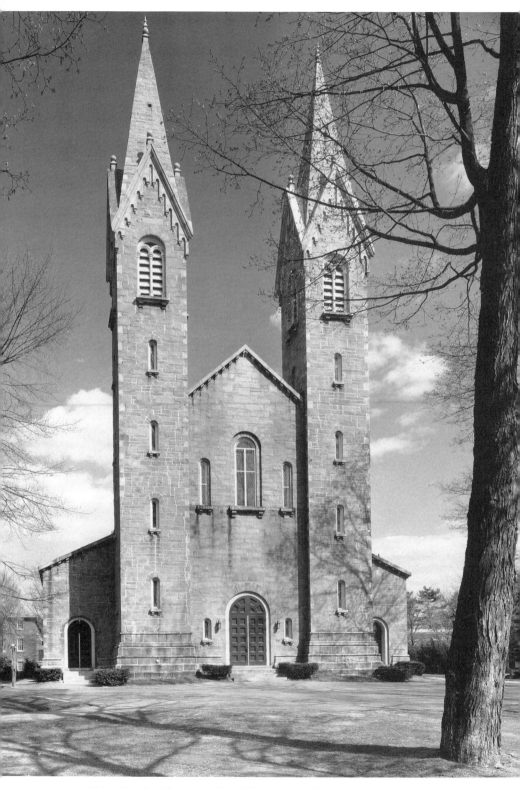

9 Richard Upjohn, Chapel, Bowdoin College, Brunswick, Maine, 1844–55, exterior (photo: Richard Cheek; courtesy of the Bowdoin College Museum of Art, Brunswick, Maine)

1871–74 in Springfield, Massachusetts, for all that its tower echoes that of William Burges and E. W. Godwin's 1866 competition project for the London Law Courts, in its balanced, single-towered silhouette, reductive ashlar walls, and dressed stone details, nonetheless was a further, if still tentative, exploration in this direction (fig. 11). As we shall see, Richardson was to draw more cogently upon the local lithic tradition in his most important mature works of the next decade.

Trinity Church *is* a triumph of design—eclectic design—a building that since its completion has ranked among the top works of architectural genius in this country. As he had in his recent project for the Connecticut State

10 H. and J. E. Billings, Boston Museum, 1845–46, Tremont Street facade (photo courtesy of the Bostonian Society, Old State House)

11 Gambrill and Richardson, Hampden County Courthouse, Springfield, Mass., 1871–74, exterior (photo courtesy the Springfield Public Library)

Capitol, Richardson here drew directly upon Ecole methodology, but here he also deployed historical forms out of the distant past that would enrich the local lithic tradition. Early thumbnail sketches for the church echo that 1863 Ecole project for a casino: on the back of the letter inviting him to compete for the commission and on various other fugitive scraps (fig. 12), the architect developed his central-plan, pyramidal-mass church by summarizing the elements of the design into a simple geometric synthesis then elaborating it without losing sight of the initial concept. Around the central point radiate the squat chancel, transepts, and nave, in the pattern of a modified Greek cross; above the central point in the finished building rises the squat tower; around these spaces Richardson wrapped French and Spanish Romanesque granite masses and details (fig. 13). The organization and stone patterning of the east end, for instance, were derived from the twelfth-century churches of the Auvergne. The central tower was inspired by that of the cathedral at Salamanca (like the Auvergnac sources known to the architect from publications in his library). And as a Romanesque pyramid, Trinity as a whole owed something to Ecole projects such as Guadet's 1864 Prix-de-Rome–winning Hospice in the Alps (see fig. 2). The result was an eclectic pile unlike any other church then standing in this country. To this day it contrasts sharply with Cummings and Sears's contemporary New Old South Church across Copley Square, an asymmetrical, polychromatic, Victorian Gothic pile of accumulated, diverse, and nervous detail. Romanesque Trinity, coherent, balanced, and serene, was Richardson's first exercise in disciplining the picturesque. It immediately distinguished the architect in his own time, and it generated an important new phase in the evolution of late nineteenth-century American architecture known as the Richardsonian Romanesque. Here Richardson had begun to create an architecture of his own.

As practiced intermittently by its originator, the Richardsonian Romanesque was in fact an alternate eclectic mode combining elements of three general styles, the bold, primitive characteristics of which were particularly attractive to him: the Syrian Early Christian, the Byzantine, and the French and Spanish Romanesque, which have in common not only semicircular openings but a fundamentally lithic murality. Richardson was to find strength in these sources, using them from Trinity onward either in combinations or, as we shall see in the next chapter, by absorbing their lessons into even more basic formal solutions to a variety of building problems. Many of Richardson's contemporaries saw his reliance upon these sources generating his most characteristic work, and they began to seek inspiration

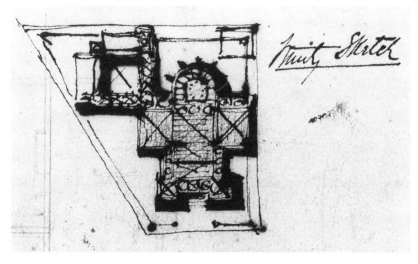

12 H. H. Richardson, Trinity Church, Boston, preliminary sketch plan, 1872 (by permission of the Houghton Library, Harvard University)

at the same fonts. Richardson's own works in the Richardsonian Romanesque range in quality from the relatively ordinary to the absolutely superb. Among the former could be included the rather lifeless Austin Hall at Harvard (1881–84) and the ponderous, overwrought Chamber of Commerce building that once stood in Cincinnati (1885–88). His unbuilt project for All Saints' Cathedral, Albany, would, if accepted, certainly have been modified, but as it survives on paper it suggests another building of studied inertness. At the other extreme, the mighty Allegheny County Courthouse in Pittsburgh (1883–88) with its attending jail ranks as one of his major achievements and is without doubt his most impressive surviving monument.

The courthouse (figs. 14–15) is lucidly organized and richly formed in keeping with its function as a public building both serviceable and ceremonial. It rests upon a 200-by-300-foot rectangular plan in which served and servant spaces are clearly defined. Wings contain primary spaces, such as the two-story, cross-ventilated courtrooms, that are separated by superimposed, one-story secondary spaces containing judges' chambers, jury rooms, consultation rooms, and so forth, and are directly accessible from a corridor surrounding a central courtyard. There are stairs at each corner of the courtyard and a main stairhall at the center of the Grant Street wing. The exterior block is marked by corner pavilions terminating symmetrical

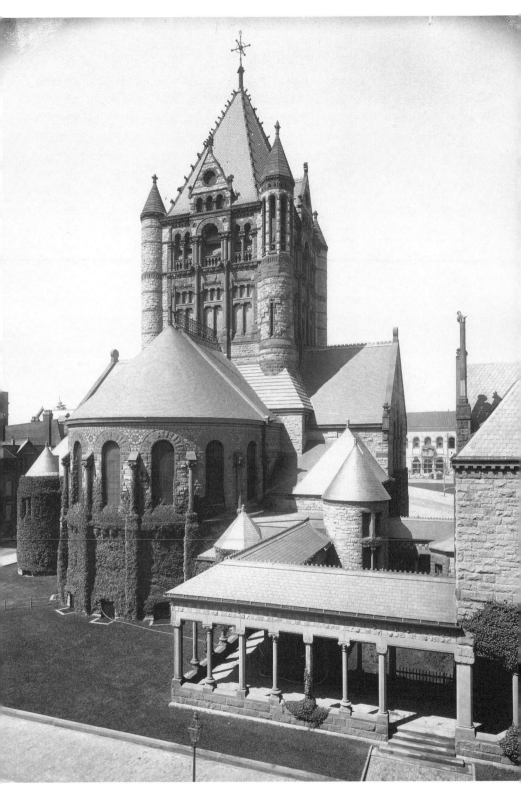

13 Gambrill and Richardson, Trinity Church, Boston, 1872–77, exterior from the northeast (photo: Baldwin Coolidge, courtesy of the Society for the Preservation of New England Antiquities)

elevations given focus by central entrances and accented on each side by a pedimented bay flanked by half-round towers and, on the Grant Street front, by the 250-foot tower over the main stair. Details are derived primarily from either Early Christian or Romanesque lithic forms. Low-sprung

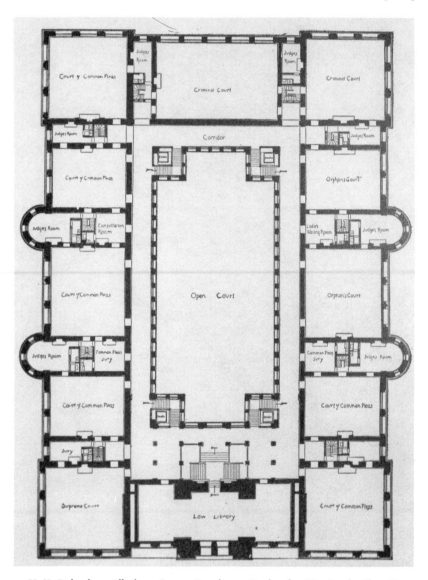

14 H. H. Richardson, Allegheny County Courthouse, Pittsburgh, 1884–87, plan (from Van Rensselaer, *Richardson*, 1888)

28

15 H. H. Richardson, Allegheny County Courthouse and Jail, exterior (photo courtesy the Boston Athenaeum)

Syrian arches built of exaggerated voussoirs of a type Richardson had seen on a brief trip to Spain in 1882 surround the entrances; Romanesque arcades mark salient features such as the courtroom level; French lucarnes extend the facades of the pavilions into the high roof area; restrained Romanesque ornament, more implied than stated, is found throughout. The main stairhall is formed by an array of semicircular stone arches smaller in size but nearly as grand as the Roman fantasies of Piranesi, whom Richardson had studied as a student in Paris.

The Pittsburgh courthouse was intended to form the focal point in the urban matrix; its central tower, which with its ancillary towers (fig. 15) served a state-of-the-art ventilating system based upon that of the Houses of Parliament in London, formed a visual exclamation point marking the civic center. Both function and symbol called for an enriched silhouette in the picturesque tradition. But the difference between this mature Richardsonian Romanesque design and the picturesqueness of his peers can be seen by comparing the courthouse with Vaux and Withers's polymorphous Jefferson Market Courthouse of the previous decade (see fig. 4). In the Pittsburgh courthouse Richardson brought a measure of discipline to the picturesque without losing any of this richness. In the words of Van Rensselaer, this is "the most magnificent and imposing of his works, yet it is the most logical and quiet."

Richardson worked in an era in which new architectural forms grew out of historical precedent. His work in his own time was distinguished in part by a choice of historical precedent that was largely unworked by his recent predecessors or his contemporaries. After Trinity he appropriated the low-sprung, heavy semicircular arch, rock-faced granite ashlar, and carved flora and fauna to a series of design problems, including the commuter railroad station, the small-town library, the monumental public building, the urban commercial block, the city residence, and a variety of other building types. The identifiable "Richardsonian Romanesque" image was established in the brief decade between the dedication of Trinity in 1877 and his death in 1886. Some of his colleagues and successors quickly began to incorporate his characteristically heavy forms into their already rich vocabulary, grafting them onto the accumulative design process with which they were familiar, to create Romanesque picturesque piles. They frequently neglected the essential discipline that marked the works of the master himself.

Boston architects, at first, and then architects across the East and Midwest, began to work within the cast of his "lengthened shadow" (to appropriate part of Emerson's definition of an institution). Their output accounts for a wealth of architectural landmarks that are more or less variations on Richardson's forms. As we would expect, the Boston-Cambridge area contains a qualitatively wide range of Richardson-inspired works such as Arthur Vinal's picturesque Chestnut Hill Pumping Station (1887) and the symmetrical Cambridge City Hall (1889) by Longfellow, Alden and Harlow. But Richardson's work had major impact on other areas of the country and especially in the burgeoning cities and towns of the Midwest. Variations on Trinity Church, for example, dot the area: Burling and Whitehouse's Trinity Church (1887) in Kansas City and Theodore Links's Second Presbyterian (1898–99) in St. Louis are but two specimens. (Seymour Davis of Kansas used only a variant of the tower, which he set upon a squashed version of a generic Richardsonian library in his project of about 1891 for a Unitarian church.) While some Richardsonian Romanesque works tend toward a restraint characteristic of the master himself at his quiet best, containing in passages if not in total a handling of broad forms and lithic materials of great distinction, many of them can only be characterized as veritable clangers. The Wichita City Hall of Proudfoot and Bird, and the County Courthouse in Waxahachie, Texas, rank among the most boisterously ludicrous.

Richardson himself thought of his monumental Pittsburgh civic center as his crowning achievement, and indeed, variations of it can be counted from Long and Kees's City Hall and Hennepin County Courthouse in Minneapolis (1888–1906) to the Old Post Office building in Washington, D.C. by Willoughby Edbrooke (1899). As we shall see, Richardson's coeval Chicago works were to have a more important historical impact upon Sullivan and Wright; but the Allegheny County buildings eventually drew even Wright's praise, and they formed the focus of one of his most extended and least equivocal notices of his predecessor. Wright was not a man to comment favorably on the works of other architects, and especially not those by the one person other than Sullivan himself who had a formative role in his early career; throughout his many publications over a long life he vacillated between passing snide remarks and brief, grudging admiration for Richardson. In a relatively long notice published in the *Capital Times* of Madison, Wisconsin, as late as 9 August 1935, however, Wright recognized, in characteristically fuzzy prose, both the Romanesque and the Richardsonian dimensions of the Pittsburgh buildings: "The courthouse and jail is [*sic*] 'Romanesque' in style only to the point where it becomes Richardsonian. Therein the building transcends the other eclecticisms that might seem, as such, to have justification for their existence. In the courthouse and jail the man was bigger than the style." In his own awkward way Wright pointed out an essential factor in our estimation of the Pittsburgh buildings and other of Richardson's best works (one so often overlooked by his imitators): that they are superb not because they are Romanesque but because they are Richardsonian. And the jail behind the courthouse is among the most impressively Richardsonian of the architect's achievements.

If the Allegheny County Courthouse itself is the finest exemplar of Richardson's own brand of eclecticism, the appended jail (fig. 15) shows to what extent he could apply force and discipline to extend the limits of architectural derivation. Here the somber program called for a treatment more restrained than that of its public-access neighbor. By the time Richardson designed the jail, the plan had become traditional for penal institutions, with cell blocks originally radiating in three directions from a central guardroom attached to an administration wing, itself connected to the courthouse by a bridge above the intervening street. The complex is secured by a high wall surrounding the site. Architecture here is basic, relying very little upon historical association, although clearly inspired by the monumental lithic architecture of earlier ages. The stern exterior is composed largely of massive, rock-faced, horizontal ashlar unrelieved from water table to coping stone. The few openings in the granite envelope are either rectangular or round-arched voids left in the stonework, or Syrian-arched entrances with extravagant, eight-foot, identical voussoirs cut with concentric intrados and extrados (fig. 16). No carved ornament is used. The result is a masterwork of elemental architecture wrought at majestic scale.

The Pittsburgh buildings embody the full range of the architect's achievement, from the Romanesque to the Richardsonian, from the eclectic to the coherent, from precedent-seeking to precedent-setting, all embodied within a disciplined design. Richardson's work was at once traditional, of its time, and forward looking. This richness led to a diversity of impact on his followers, from the adequate Romanesque pastiches of an Edward T. Potter to the extraordinary extrapolations of a Frank Lloyd Wright, as they sought within his lavish accomplishments fodder for their own aims. Richardson's aim, judging from his works (for he never expressed it in words), was much like that of his contemporaries and followers such as McKim, Mead and White: to embody the best of the European past in seeking solutions for the programs of the present. But, where McKim and company sought to express American architecture as the latest phase of an ongoing classical tradition (the architect Thomas Hastings wrote in 1897, "we are still living in . . . the Renaissance"), Richardson tried to adapt traditional stone architecture to a specifically American imagery.

16 H. H. Richardson, Allegheny County Jail, detail of exterior (photo: author)

If European-trained, cosmopolite Richardson harbored thoughts of creating an architecture distinct from its European sources, an architecture corresponding to his reading of the American society of his time, those
thoughts must have come to him through the circle of New England intellectuals, some of whom were his friends, clients, and colleagues. Emerson
had long ago issued a call for a national culture generated by an individual
self-reliance. "Insist on yourself; never imitate," he had written in 1841.
Among the most important of those intellectuals closer to Richardson was
the landscape architect and environmental theorist, Richardson's friend,
neighbor, and erstwhile collaborator, Frederick Law Olmsted. It was probably from Olmsted that Richardson came to sense the transformations in
American society that were creating the concentric urban pattern of the
1880s, with urban commercial core and suburban domestic rings all connected by the radiating commuter railroad system. Revived Romanesque
forms might do for traditional building types, such as educational buildings, churches, courthouses, and chambers of commerce; but the new or

evolving types born of the new or evolving social patterns, especially the urban commercial block and the detached, single-family house, as well as the commuter depot and small-town public library, required more imaginative responses. As Emerson had concluded in his essay "Art" (1841), "it is in vain that we look for genius to reiterate its miracles in the old arts; it is its instinct to find beauty . . . in the field and roadside, in the shop and mill." That Olmsted and others thought this applied to Richardson's ultimate achievement is suggested by the fact that Van Rensselaer's monograph on the architect, a work of 1888 sponsored in part by the landscape architect, bears as epigraph on its title page the lines immediately preceding these from Emerson's essay. That Richardson did indeed find inspiration not only in the stone architectures of Europe but in the American mill and in the American field will soon become apparent. For in seeking appropriate forms for city and suburb, for market and domicile, he was to add to his beloved round-arched lithic sources those which he could plausibly identify as indigenous to or developed within the American context. By 1880, as we shall see, he was ready to draw upon these sources as he attempted to create an American architecture distinct from its European background.

2

BUILDINGS FOR CITY AND SUBURB

17 Gambrill and Richardson, Oliver Ames Memorial Library, North Easton, Mass., 1877–79, exterior of alcove wing (from Van Rensselaer, *Richardson*, 1888)

In the spring of 1874, H. H. Richardson moved from Staten Island to Brookline, a suburb of Boston, presumably to be closer to his growing New England practice and his and his wife's social connections. He rented an early nineteenth-century house from his old friend E. W. "Ned" Hooper and established his workroom in a downstairs parlor. Gradually during the following years he installed his growing number of assistants in one-story sheds stretching backward from the house. Richardson's was an unusual setting for an American architect of the time: in Brookline his helpers and his family (eventually including six children) freely intermingled, with each feeling that he or she had a place in his work. It was an integration of

35

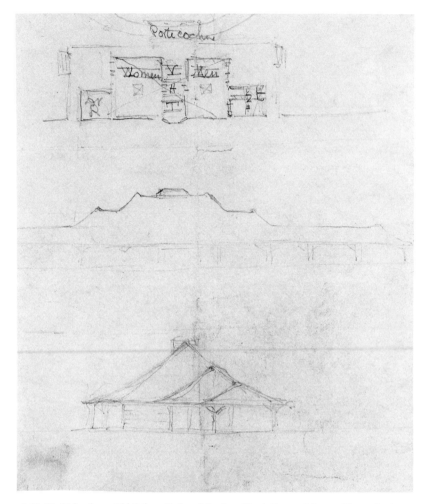

18 H. H. Richardson, Old Colony Railroad Station, North Easton, Mass., 1881, preliminary sketch (by permission of the Houghton Library, Harvard University)

personal and professional life that was later to find a parallel in Frank Lloyd Wright's establishments in Oak Park in the 1890s and at Taliesin after 1911. From this studio in Brookline during the last twelve years of his life Richardson turned out the mature works upon which his reputation primarily rests.

Richardson's written theoretical statements were few and brief and were concerned with elements such as wall, mass, void, and the relationship between the three. Beyond this he spoke of repose, of quietude, as his ultimate goal. He expressed no interest in the new materials and structural innovations of his time. He and his builder, O. W. Norcross of Norcross Brothers, rarely incorporated them into his works (although after Richardson's death Norcross was concerned with such innovative techniques as flat-slab concrete construction). These few expressed preferences give the historian little guidance, but when they are checked against his buildings, they become important guides in our understanding of Richardson's mature aims in relation to the work of his peers. He sought to muffle the shrillness of the contemporary picturesque with a disciplined approach to plan, mass, the relationship of solids and voids, and the handling of details, all within a conservative structural approach. He wanted a "quiet and massive" architecture. The best projected and executed buildings of his last decade permit us to see these principles in action, and they also permit us to go beyond his written remarks in our characterization of his aims and his achievement.

19 H. H. Richardson, Old Colony Railroad Station, 1881–84, exterior (photo: Cervin Robinson for Historic American Building Survey)

As a youth, Richardson experienced the controlled quietude that characterized the hip-roofed antebellum architecture of southern Louisiana, the granite architecture of the Boston-Cambridge area (see fig. 10), and such prizewinning French work as Guadet's Alpine hospice (fig. 2). As a mature designer, he imposed that element of quietude right from the beginning of a project, by the design method he acquired at the Ecole. The *esquisse* established initial control over a multipartite building program, its coherent geometry guiding all subsequent development of a design in both plan and three dimensions. This effect is seen in the series of sketches for Trinity Church (fig. 12), in sketches for the Oliver Ames House project of 1880, for the Albany City Hall of 1880, for the Crane Memorial Library at Quincy, Massachusetts, of 1880, and for the Albany Cathedral of 1882; but the definitive example that emerges from Richardson's graphic remains is the design of the Old Colony Railway Depot at North Easton, Massachusetts, 1881 (fig. 18). In a characteristically small, orthographic sketch on blue stationery, Richardson lightly penciled the plan and two elevations of a simple shelter containing men's and women's waiting rooms, ticket office, baggage room, and toilet, all axially arranged beneath a harboring hip roof that spreads over a porte cochere on one side and into a trackside shed on the other. In the long, middle elevation he pressed down heavily in going over the roof ridge as if to impose by the push of the pencil a controlling order on the mass. Similar intent seems evident in an elevation of about 1880 for an unidentified suburban house in which Richardson sketched elements such as the eaves, slopes, and ridge of the roof in pencil and then punched them up in ink.

A second set of sketches for the Old Colony Depot, in brown ink over pencil on tracing paper, suggests that Richardson was dissatisfied with the many jogs in his initial plan that resulted in the double hip roof, confusing the end elevation. In these later studies he sketched a simple rectangular plan, retaining the axial organization of spaces and graphically demonstrating the flow of traffic from porte cochere through lobby around ticket office to trackside platform, and then firmed up the drawing with inked emphasis. The evolved, simplified plan exhibits greater control of the program and generates, in a related, ink-over-graphite perspective rare among Richardson's surviving drawings, a simplified three-dimensional mass controlled by a unifying hip roof. This depot (fig. 19) is erected as a point of transition between the machinery of the railroad on the one side and, on the other, the greenery of Olmsted's picturesque landscape at Langwater, the F. L. Ames estate, a vista of which is framed by the single arch of the porte cochere.

20 Frank Furness and Allen Evans, Philadelphia and Reading Railroad Depot, Graver's Lane, Chestnut Hill, Pa., before 1884, exterior (photo: Cervin Robinson)

The station's broadly proportioned silhouette (originally even broader when the hip roof spread into the trackside shed), sturdy half-circular arches springing from the ground, massive sandstone-trimmed, random ashlar walls with very wide rectangular openings, and horizontally spreading ridge and eaves altogether produce a visual repose that is in marked contrast to, say, the actively accretive, contemporary commuter depots of Frank Furness, such as that at Graver's Lane, Chestnut Hill, Pennsylvania (fig. 20).

Richardson's use of the *esquisse* led from rational analysis to disciplined synthesis in the representative examples cited above; the same process also occurred in a series of designs generated by a series of related building programs. The oft-remarked evolution of the Richardsonian library, for example, begins at the Winn Memorial in Woburn, Massachusetts (1876–79), with an analysis of the program requiring reading room, book storage, art gallery, and natural history museum, plus ancillary spaces (fig. 21). As built, these discrete spaces are loosely joined along main and secondary cross axes and rise in three dimensions to a dramatically irregular and

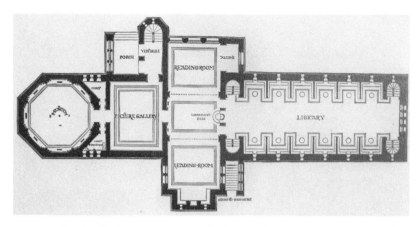

21 Gambrill and Richardson, Winn Memorial Library, Woburn, Mass., 1876–79, plan (from Van Rensselaer, *Richardson*, 1888)

22 Gambrill and Richardson, Winn Memorial Library, exterior (photo: Jean Baer O'Gorman)

asymmetrical potpourri of forms, materials, colors, and textures (fig. 22). The rectangular alcove wing collides with the transverse, gabled reading room block unbalanced by the gawky stair tower wedged between it and the pinched, segmentally arched entry, with an octagonal, clerestoried museum with high pitched roof tacked on the opposite end. This is one of Richardson's last thoroughly picturesque works, its additive composition not only the result of analysis left unsynthesized but of detail bumping detail without an overarching order. Here Richardson still thought in parts. By the time he designed the Crane Memorial in Quincy, however, he was thinking of the whole (fig. 23). In the series of surviving plan sketches he gradually achieved synthesis, and the resulting building is the essence of quiet and massive architecture. Embellishment on such a commemorative building was essential in an era guided by John Ruskin's "Lamp of Sacrifice" in *The Seven Lamps of Architecture* (1849; a work Richardson owned), but the Romanesque details are completely subordinate to the interweaving of its

23 H. H. Richardson, Crane Memorial Library, Quincy, Mass., 1880–82, exterior (photo courtesy the Boston Athenaeum)

elemental tectonic forms: roof, wall, gable, arch, and tower, and the reiterative horizontal that generates the aura of order and repose.

The integration Richardson achieved in the compact, synthetic plans of the libraries at North Easton, Quincy, and elsewhere in small suburban towns around Boston produces open interiors covered by beamed or barrel-vaulted ceilings and subdivided by two-story book alcoves (fig. 24). It is carried to the exterior in Richardson's organization of the masses of these

24 Gambrill and Richardson, Ames Memorial Library, North Easton, Mass., interior (*Monographs of American Architecture*, 3; photo courtesy the Society for the Preservation of New England Antiquities)

buildings into tripartite horizontal zones (fig. 17). From bottom to top there are: a broad, solid, ashlar base resting upon a water table, a horizontal strip of identical openings edged by continuous sill and lintel usually of contrasting stone or workmanship, and a spreading gable or hip roof, occasionally (as at Quincy) enlivened but not interrupted by subtle, eyebrow dormers, and usually edged with contrasting ridge tiles to emphasize its level termination against the sky. Although these stacked horizontal zones are usually interrupted visually by the gabled salient that contains the entrance archway, belt courses and inferential continuity imply their controlling presence even when they are not actually there (see fig. 23). These main horizontal zones are reinforced by lesser horizontal accents repeated from top to bottom of the libraries as well as other of Richardson's mature works. These are the essential keys to his disciplining of the picturesque to achieve an architecture of repose.

The processes just examined move from complex to simple. Richardson's development as a whole was marked by the elimination of many of the attributes of the picturesque, a direction that might have resulted in an overly disciplined, lifeless architecture had he not retained just enough variety to quicken his quieted forms. In time, carved ornament derived largely from Romanesque or Byzantine sources or from Ruskin's works became less evident in his mature commissions. Gradually he shifted from a polychromatic, random ashlar granite with contrasting sandstone trim, as at Trinity Church or the Ames (fig. 17) or Crane libraries, to monochromatic horizontal ashlar with no contrasting trim, as at the Allegheny County Jail (fig. 16), the Marshall Field store, or the Glessner House (fig. 34), to name just three. Increasingly he pushed forms together, building one broad dormer at Sever Hall, Harvard University (1878–80), where initial sketches show two or more; creating arches of identical voussoirs, from Trinity Church on, where he had earlier used the alternating stones common among his contemporaries; or creating tightly contained silhouettes in most of his mature works. His major interior spaces, such as in Trinity Church, the Senate Chamber in Albany, or the libraries (fig. 24), achieve serenity, or as he expressed it, "simplicity and quietness," through his use of broad, harmonious proportions and coordinated materials and colors. These were the salient characteristics of Richardson's mature, disciplined style, and, as his assistant W. P. P. Longfellow put it in the 12 March 1887 issue of the *American Architect and Building News,* "wherever it prevails it extinguishes the fantastic as a rising tide puts out fire."

But Richardson also knew how to create within his disciplined approach that "living architecture" he had aspired to build from the moment he re-turned from France. He controlled but did not forsake the richness of sur-face that characterized the works of his peers. One device he appropriated from the picturesque but made his own was the interplay between symme-try and asymmetry that marks, for example, both plan and massing of James Renwick's Smithsonian Institution on the Mall in Washington, D.C. (1846–49). In some cases he set up a symmetrical pattern and then upset it by introducing an asymmetrical element; in other cases he placed an asym-metrical grouping within a regular mass. The former arrangement occurs, for example, in the eastern elevation of Trinity Parish House (fig. 25), where the symmetrical pattern established by ground-floor arcade and cen-tered lucarne above is unbalanced by the addition of a variant bay to the north, and again in the Prairie Avenue facade of the Glessner House (fig. 34), where the balanced arrangement centered on the main entrance is upset by the carriageway to the left and the openings above it. The latter arrange-ment occurs in the juxtaposition of archway and stair tower within the ga-bled salient at the Crane Library (fig. 23), or in the pairing of polygonal and round towers in the Paine House in Waltham, Massachusetts (1884–87; see fig. 41). But the interplay between symmetry and asymmetry extended into details as well. Richardson, or his customary builder, Norcross Broth-ers, saw to it that ashlar patterns were rarely symmetrical in identical areas flanking an axis. (It is possible to tell a Richardson building from one by an imitator on the basis of this one detail alone: on the Post Office building opposite the Ames Memorial Hall in North Easton, Massachusetts, a post-1900 work by Shepley, Rutan and Coolidge, the pattern of stonework to the right of the central axis mirrors that to the left.)

By 1880 Richardson was in full control of his formal means. Over and over again he created orderly plans rising into orderly but vital masses ar-ticulated by a superb rendering of the basic elements of his art. A gable or hip roof hovered overhead, gathering the layered forms below into a quiet silhouette. Walls were usually of ashlar detailed to suggest thickness; brick was less common and shingles marked many residential works. Openings, whether trabeated or arcuated, were broad and generous. The horizontal predominated. These characteristics more or less mark all of his mature buildings, but they are found over and over again in the depots mainly for the Boston and Albany line and in the libraries for small towns ringing Boston.

Richardson built for nearly all aspects of contemporary American soci-ety, providing solutions to religious, educational, commercial, civic, trans-

25 Gambrill and Richardson, Trinity Parish House, Boston, east elevation (photo: author)

portation, domestic, recreational, commemorative, medical, and governmental programs. According to John J. Glessner's "The Story of a House" (1923), the architect boasted of a willingness to design anything a client wanted, "from a cathedral to a chicken coop." Among his mature works, however, there are four building types that carry the weight of his achievement: the suburban library, the commuter depot, the commercial block, and the detached single-family house. Richardson gave these four building types his indelible stamp in the brief decade between the dedication of Trinity Church and his death, and they were building types associated with the historical transformations in American society that occurred with quickening pace in the years following the Civil War.

These types can be plotted on the radiating pattern of American urban development during these years: the commercial block is a central urban form, the library and depot belong to the suburban towns ringing the commercial center, and the home might be located anywhere along the radius from inner city through suburbia to exurbia. Like massiveness and quietude, function and location were formative factors in Richardson's solutions to these building problems. Drawing upon the environmental vision of his erstwhile collaborator Frederick Law Olmsted, Richardson seems to have attempted to generate architectural forms appropriate to their content and their context, that is, their position within contemporary society. In so

45

26 H. H. Richardson, Marshall Field Wholesale Store, Chicago, 1885–87, exterior (from *Inland Architect*, 1888; photo courtesy of the Art Institute of Chicago)

doing he was to create prototypes for urban commercial and suburban or rural domestic buildings that were to inspire, among other subsequent works, the office buildings of Louis Sullivan and the residences of Frank Lloyd Wright.

Because Richardson died during its construction, the Marshall Field Wholesale Store in Chicago (1885–87; fig. 26) was his culminating statement of urban commercial form, but it was also the result of previous experiment. It was his last solution to a building type the external articulation of which had concerned him throughout his career. If we exclude Richardson's early and bookish essays in commercial design, such as the Western Railway Offices at Springfield, Massachusetts (1867–69), we can point to the Hayden Building he erected in 1875 for his father-in-law's estate as the beginning of his search for what he considered a suitable expression of American urban commerce (fig. 27). In the facades of the Hayden Building Richardson made a clear connection to Boston's commercial granite style in his use of the dressed stone itself as the unit of design and in the clear, building-block detailing of the piers, arches, and lintels. He also began to integrate the design by using tall arches to bind the third and fourth floors. In fact, the pattern of superimposed trabeated and arcuated openings on the upper three floors of the narrow Washington Street front directly anticipates the upper three floors of the Field facades. But elsewhere his design is tentative: on the long La Grange Street side, openings are irregularly spaced and the alignment of trabeated and arcuated voids is faulty.

The Cheney Building in Hartford of the same year is larger and therefore a more imposing urban presence. The main facade of the five-story block is divided into three horizontal tiers, the first with five broad arches embracing two floors, the second with a two-story arcade of ten primary openings, the third a one-story arcade of fourteen openings between corner pavilions. While its geometric integration is an improvement over the side elevation of the Hayden, in fact the Cheney facade visually disintegrates into asymmetrical corners, alternating voussoirs of the arches, additive aedicules over the entrances, and richly carved belt courses and capitals. It is the work of a designer who has not yet achieved a clarity of purpose. The Ames Wholesale Store in Boston (1882–83) seems a restudy of the Cheney aimed at accomplishing a better integration of superimposed arcades without the asymmetrical, polychromatic enrichment of the earlier work. Below the cornice the result is serene; above, the building disintegrates into a disarray of pointed lucarnes. Here too the designer seems to be at odds with himself.

At the Marshall Field Wholesale Store (fig. 26) these various experiments come together to form a perfect whole. Richardson drew here upon Romanesque and Renaissance models, his own earlier commercial works, the granite style of midcentury Boston, and the early industrial buildings of New England, to create a massive but integrated building that set a new standard for commercial order and individual urban scale within the center of Chicago. As it came just at the culmination of a technological revolution that was to spawn the metal-framed skyscraper, it is necessary to emphasize

27 Gambrill and Richardson, Hayden Building, Boston, 1875–76, exterior (photo: Jean Baer O'Gorman)

that, despite the apparent incorporation of some iron into the fabric in the form of box girders above first-floor window heads (fig. 28), Richardson and Norcross here relied upon traditional load-bearing structure. For Richardson, the design problem handed him must have seemed one of establishing the proper look for an urban building to meet the relatively uncomplicated needs of the wholesale half of a great mercantile enterprise. That he succeeded in the eyes of contemporaries we learn from Sullivan's characterization in "The Oasis" or from statements such as that of John Edelmann, a Chicago architect who early made an impression on Sullivan, who called it "massive, simple, brutal, naive, a true expression of its inward character." As Edelmann was a socialist, he had little admiration for the capitalist aspect of that character, but he could recognize the force of the expression as clearly as anyone else.

For Marshall Field's wholesale establishment, Richardson provided a stack of floors supported by the exterior walls and a regular interior grid of columns and girders. In the center of the rear of the block was an indentation forming a loading dock at ground level. The indentation was surrounded by brick walls reduced to a virtual skeleton by the profusion of windows with segmental heads. In the treatment of these largely hidden, utilitarian planes Richardson drew upon the characteristic facade pattern of the traditional New England mill. In his internal structural system, he also adopted in part the heavy-timber, fire-resistant construction developed for these same early industrial buildings. Richardson's partial reliance here on the ubiquitous manufacturing buildings of his adopted New England recalls Emerson's statement in "Art" about the mundane origins of the new American beauty in "shop and mill." Richardson's Brookline neighbor, the fire insurance expert Edward Atkinson, would call the Field store a "glorified cotton factory."

The main facades were more monumental and apparently more heavily dependent on European precedent, although they might be as well defined as extensions of the mid-nineteenth-century Boston granite tradition (see fig. 10). They were composed of ruddy sandstone and granite divided into a base, a three-story arcade, a two-story arcade, and a trabeated upper floor. One must search closely in surviving photographs of this demolished building, as presumably one might have had to scrutinize the building itself, for the occasional bits and pieces of carved ornament of vaguely Romanesque inspiration (two fragments in the Graham Foundation collection are all that survive of this huge block). As Richardson worked on the Field store, he told a reporter from the *Chicago Tribune* that he had "long had certain ideas

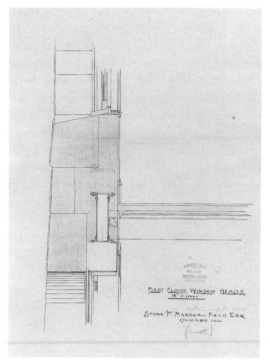

28 Office of H. H. Richardson (or Norcross Brothers), Marshall Field Wholesale Store, section through first-floor window heads (photo courtesy of the Houghton Library, Harvard University)

he wished to embody in such a building." These involved "the beauty of material and symmetry rather than of mere superficial ornamentation." The building was to be "plain . . . , the effects depending on the relations of the 'voids and solids,' . . . on the proportion of the parts." He was to achieve here a complete integration of horizontals and verticals within an apparently rectangular solid, without the interrupting belt courses, the picturesque asymmetries and chromatics, or the unruly skylines of his earlier, tentative experiments. The monumental exterior of the Field store was the fullest realization of his search for a "massive and quiet" architecture for urban commercial America.

The building radiated a congruence of commercial purpose and architectural expression scarcely rivaled in its day. Richardson achieved this result by relying upon traditional architectural imagery: the quattrocento palace and the Boston granite commercial style. He also achieved it within traditional structural forms. Although iron box girders were apparently used as lintels to reinforce the basement window heads (fig. 28), the main facades were load-bearing masonry piles and articulated as such (see fig. 26). A section through a window head reveals to what extent Richardson hid his reliance upon the advantages of metal. How distinctly different it is from a section through the wall of a slightly later Chicago structure, Burnham and Root's Reliance Building of 1890. The Reliance is a frame building covered with terra-cotta and infilled with glass. Its section, like its three-dimensional form (see fig. 60), reveals the actual and visual lightness inherent in the structural system (fig. 29), a lightness that gave rise to the skyscraper of the twentieth-century American city. There is no correspondence between these two sectional details, just as there was no direct connection between Richardson's horizontal, wall-bearing Field store and the rise of the steel-framed skyscraper, although there is a direct connection between the store and Louis Sullivan's attempts to come to terms with urban commercial design.

Now that the Field store and the physical character of central Chicago in the 1880s have disappeared, we must make an heroic effort to understand how Sullivan and other contemporary architects saw the one against the

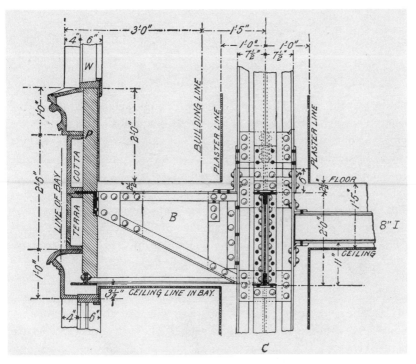

29 Burnham and Root, Reliance Building, Chicago, 1890, structural section of a window bay (from Jordy, *American Buildings and Their Architects*, 1972)

30 Office of H. H. Richardson, Marshall Field Wholesale Store, preliminary perspective (photo courtesy of the Houghton Library, Harvard University)

backdrop of the other. The Field store was a simple and unified solid occupying an entire block. Most street fronts in Chicago during this decade were composed of a variety of buildings on lots of various widths designed by a variety of architects for a variety of purposes. The result was an accretive streetscape visually composed of bits and pieces, the extension into the urban dimension of the eclectic compositional format of the individual picturesque building. That the architect had this contrast in mind is suggested by the perspective sketch of the building that survives among his graphic remains (fig. 30). Richardson and his office seldom used such perspective studies, preferring to envision buildings in isolated orthography according to the Ecole method, but the Field store set into the center of Chicago suggested another approach. With rapid strokes of crayon and brush, leaving much to the imagination of the viewer, the unnamed draftsman showed the ruddy solid within a thick tangle of black slashes. He thus captured the essential characteristic of the finished blockbuster: that it was literally outstanding, a landmark or promontory, within a picturesque environment. And so Sullivan described it in "The Oasis."

31 H. H. Richardson, Ames Harrison Avenue Store, Boston, 1886–88, exterior (*American Architect and Building News*, 1887; photo courtesy Jeffrey K. Ochsner)

The Field store was Richardson's definitive urban design; but at the very end of his life, his office produced in the F. L. Ames Store on Harrison Avenue in Boston (1886–87) a six-story commercial building that, although not itself of skeletal construction, has seemed to some recent observers to presage the skeletal design of later work. The exterior walls were brick above a one-story, traditional Boston granite base, with five-story glazing beneath broad arches resting upon relatively thin piers (fig. 31). This design was published nationally in 1887. While its vertically articulated exterior and crisp detailing have seemed more proto-Sullivanesque than the Field store, it is difficult to assess the Harrison Avenue store in the light of other office work. It is doubtful that the architect himself approved of anything more than the first-floor plans he mentioned in a letter just six weeks before his death, so responsibility for the final product is unclear. What is clear is that this design stands out from anything that went before or came after it in the office. The subsequent work of his successors, Shepley, Rutan and Coolidge, such as their thirteen-story Ames Building on Court Street in Boston (1889–91), is a distant relative of both the Field and the Harrison Avenue stores. This wall-bearing masonry building, in which a four-story arcade is set upon a high arcuated base, suggests a mass gouged by Romanesque openings (fig. 32). From the lightness of Harrison Avenue the office here returned to the weightiness of the Field store.

Richardson's residential works were commissioned for city, suburb, and country, and for each he generated an appropriately different image. During his mature years he created a series of urbane houses for the city, culminating in the John J. Glessner House in Chicago. The series begins with the assured rectory for Trinity Church in Boston's Back Bay (1879–80), a building of hard red brick and brownstone with cavernous arched entry that centers the symmetrical-asymmetrical interplay of solids and voids so characteristic of his lively disciplined style. The rectory was followed by townhouses for F. L. Higginson, also in Back Bay (1881–82), and for Grange Sard, Jr., in Albany (1882), works that have seemed less assured to most Richardson scholars. That these richly wrought houses were aberrant efforts is suggested, however, by the austere brick mass of the N. L. Anderson House in Washington, D.C. (1881–83), the larger and sterner John Hay House in the same city (1884–86), its neighbor, the house of Henry Adams (1884–86; the embellishment of whose ground floor may reflect Adams's intervention in the design), and the coeval granite houses in Chicago for Franklin MacVeagh and John Glessner. Whether in brick or in stone, these and other, less successful city houses of the 1880s rely largely upon elemen-

32 Shepley, Rutan and Coolidge, Ames Court Street Building, Boston, 1888–89, exterior
(photo: author)

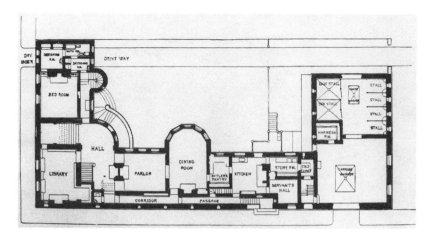

33 H. H. Richardson, John J. Glessner House, Chicago, 1885–87, plan (from Van Rensselaer, *Richardson*, 1888)

34 H. H. Richardson, Glessner House, exterior (photo: George Glessner, courtesy of the Chicago Architecture Foundation)

tal materials and masses for their architectural effect and are therefore highly characteristic of Richardson's aims.

The Glessner residence (figs. 33–35) is to Richardson's urban houses what the Field store was to his commercial work. Here this civic domestic series achieves its logical culmination. The plan is an L with its re-entrant angle turned away from the intersection of Prairie Avenue and Eighteenth Street. Within, the main hall with stair and fireplace is tucked into the angle. This circulatory space divides the library from the parlor, on the other side of which is the rectangular dining room with fireplace opposite a polygonal bay extending beyond the block. Externally, the austere outer walls of monochromatic granite laid in horizontal ashlar are set tightly against the public walks so that the angle shelters a private garden within its defensive shell. The inner garden walls are brick with limestone trim, thus forming a shift in texture and scale from the outer walls that marks

35 H. H. Richardson, Glessner House, court (photo courtesy of the Chicago Architecture Foundation)

57

the difference between public and private aspects. As we shall see, this and other characteristics of the Glessner residence were to have a notable impact on the first works of Frank Lloyd Wright.

For the suburbs and seashore such urbane masonry residences would have been out of place. Here Richardson joined his contemporaries in practicing the more relaxed, more appropriately scaled shingle style, the American equivalent of the English Queen Anne, in which granite, brick, and terra-cotta gave way on the exterior to shingle, that traditional New World forest equivalent of the manufactured tile of England; and interiors were often marked by a revival of colonial New England paneling and other details. Richardson's residences of the middle 1870s, from the William Watts Sherman House in Newport on, were designs that reflect the major intervention of his assistant Stanford White and are closely modeled on the contemporary work of Shaw and Nesfield in England. In plan, rooms are freely grouped around large "living halls" containing staircase and fireplace. On the exterior an assortment of forms are built of brick, stone, or shingle, and embellished with carved ornament, pargetting, or decorative half-timbering. Multiple tall chimneys vie with a multitude of pronounced gables against the sky to give a thoroughly picturesque effect. Such a work was the James Cheney House project of 1878.

With the John Bryant House at Cohasset, Massachusetts (1880–81), a work designed after White's departure, a greater regularity was imposed upon the plan, the shingles stretched continuously over walls and roof, and the individual forms were pulled into a nearly continuous exterior. Applied decorative embellishment was omitted entirely. Other major works in the shingled suburban domestic series were the Percy Browne House at Marion, Massachusetts (1881–82), the house for Mrs. M. F. Stoughton in Cambridge, Massachusetts (1882–83), the Walter Channing House in Brookline (1883–84), and the Henry Potter House in St. Louis (1886–87; figs. 36–37). Of these the Stoughton and the Potter are undoubtedly the culminating designs, but the gawky late Bigelow house in Newton, Massachusetts (1886–87), at least in plan, was particularly responsive to its site atop Oak Hill. The singled forms wrap around a courtyard and culminate in the house with belvedere, from which sweeping views were possible. Here, as in the Paine house in Waltham, Richardson seems closest to the romantic siting that marks the American country house from Thomas Jefferson (at least) through the works of Andrew Jackson Downing and Alexander Jackson Davis to Frederic Church's Olana and other Hudson River villas.

The Stoughton House is, like the later Glessner, an L-shaped building on a corner lot; but in this less urban location the building is set at the rear of a lawn (later walled) and the re-entrant angle is turned toward the public intersection in a more welcoming gesture. The characteristic shingle-style living hall with its stair and fireplace is placed in the center of the plan, with parlor and library to the left, and dining and kitchen areas to the right. On the exterior, unadorned shingled membranes course and swell around and above these inner volumes and those of the second floor and the attic. Broad, double-hung windows, some of them joined into double or even triple horizontal groupings, punctuate the shingled planes. Continuous horizontal lines ranging in emphasis from the edges of the shingles to the flared water table, pronounced eaves, and roof ridge bind the subtly differentiated forms into one continuous whole. We need only compare this quiet work with a similar contemporary building, for example the Robert Goelet House in Newport by McKim, Mead and White (1882–83; two of the partners former assistants of Richardson), with its multiple forms and added ornament, to measure the extent of Richardson's imposition of formal discipline.

The Potter House too stood on a corner lot and assumed with its stables an L-shaped plan (figs. 36–37). The living quarters, however, were in fact one room deep and aligned along one axis opposed by offset cross axes situating a polygonal stair tower on the side toward the street and the dining room extending by means of a semicircular bay into the garden opposite. On the exterior, walls and roof were wrapped in continuous wood shingles. Richardson's characteristic horizontality, coherence, and elemental architectural expression would go no further than this. The Potter House culminated the architect's shingled suburban domestic work and stood before its unfortunate demolition in 1958 as one of the best examples of an American architecture he could justly call his own.

For another group of suburban and exurban domestic works after 1880 Richardson turned away from the shingle style common to his contemporaries to an even more personal imagery he seems to have developed in order to create architectural forms in even greater harmony with the American landscape. These houses seem shaped, at least partially, as geological analogies. This group of three works, the Ames Gate Lodge at Langwater in North Easton, Massachusetts (1880–81; fig. 38), the addition to the Robert Treat Paine House in Waltham, Massachusetts (1883–87; see figs. 41–43)—in fact an awkward combination of elements including the geological and the shingled—and the E. W. Gurney House at Pride's Crossing, Massachusetts (1884–86) are all located in picturesque settings. They followed

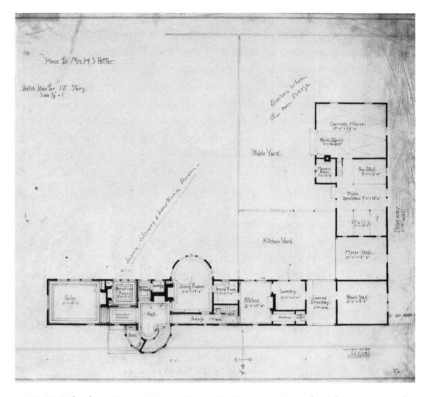

36 H. H. Richardson, Henry S. Potter House, St. Louis, 1886–87, plan (photo courtesy of the Houghton Library, Harvard University)

Richardson's creation of the Ames Monument in Wyoming in the form of a "man-made mountain" set into a spectacular geological landscape. In these works Richardson seems to have been closely inspired by the landscape architect Frederick Law Olmsted as well as by the photographic and painted imagery generated in this age of exploration and by the publications issued in the fledgling study of geology (taught at Harvard during Richardson's undergraduate days by charismatic Louis Agassiz). In these works wherever possible Richardson seems to have abandoned architectural history for natural history in an attempt to find an architecture appropriate to America in having borrowed its essential materials and forms from the American landscape. In these works he created buildings rooted in place. In these works he seems to have responded to Emerson's call for an American beauty to arise not only from the "shop and mill," as he had downtown, but from the "field and roadside."

In fact, of course, Richardson did have something of an American architectural tradition to draw upon in creating these works, just as he could build upon the Boston granite style at the Field store. If we can think of Richardson as an erstwhile associate of Olmsted, we can think of the pair as legatees of the earlier collaboration between author and landscapist Andrew Jackson Downing and architect Alexander Jackson Davis. In Downing's books, beginning with his celebrated *Treatise on the Theory and Practice of Landscape Gardening, Adapted to North America* (1841), and in some of Davis's many medieval-inspired residential designs, the pair created a climate of environmental ideas in which architecture and landscape are conceived of as a continuity (fig. 39). These were ideas born in England in the eighteenth century, which Downing and Davis naturalized during the middle of the nineteenth. And they were ideas that continued to shape the architectural program of Olmsted and Richardson. The English picturesque garden was filled with the rockeries, grottoes, and follies that form the remote ancestry of the Ames Gate Lodge; but the only earlier American building to which the Gate Lodge might conceivably be compared is Davis's

37 H. H. Richardson, Potter House, exterior (from Bryant, *Missouri's Contribution to American Architecture*, 1928; photo: Missouri Historical Society), courtesy Jeffrey K. Ochsner

38 H. H. Richardson, F. L. Ames Gate Lodge, North Easton, Mass., 1880–81, exterior (photo: author's collection)

39 Andrew Jackson Downing, "The Picturesque" (from *Theory and Practice of Landscape Gardening*, 1841)

gate lodge at Llewellyn Park in West Orange, New Jersey (ca. 1860; fig. 40). This round, fieldstone structure, nearly devoid of historical reference, fronts a picturesque garden suburb and seems in a general way to anticipate at least the rounded potting-shed end of the Ames Gate Lodge. But Richardson was to go beyond even this extraordinary compromise between architecture and nature.

The gate lodge at North Easton contains bachelor's quarters and rooms for the help to the right of the arch, as seen from the outside road, and the potting shed or orangery to the left. It is without doubt a man-made object: some of the most subtle of Richardson's architectural details are to be found in the colorful, dressed voussoirs of the main arch, in the echoing curve of the overhead eave and the re-echoing swell of the eyebrow dormer in the roof above, in the juxtaposition of unworked glacial boulders and cut sandstone trim, and in the row of continuous windows above the stone base and beneath the eave on the south side of the potting shed. But it also draws important clues from nature. At the base of the well tower on the south of

40 Alexander Jackson Davis, Gate Lodge, Llewellyn Park, West Orange, N.J., ca. 1860, exterior (photo: author's collection)

41 H. H. Richardson, Robert T. Paine House, Waltham Mass., 1883–86, exterior after 1989 restoration (photo: Richard Cheek)

the living quarters is an arch of split stone voussoirs in which geometry and geology seem to merge, and the exterior walls of naturally rounded boulders rise above an irregular plan as if to imitate a glacial moraine in a landscape designed by Olmsted, who did indeed lay out the grounds of the estate.

Richardson used this same geological analogy in the Paine House addition (figs. 41–43) and Gurney houses. In the recently restored Paine House, the towers of glacial stone flanking the side of the addition toward the vista might vaguely recall a generic French chateau; but one is polygonal and the other round, and they are set into an asymmetrical composition. Comparison of this lively arrangement with the balanced, cone-topped towers of such contemporary chateauesque designs as McKim, Mead and White's Casino at Narragansett Pier, Rhode Island (1881–84), or Richard Morris

64

42 H. H. Richardson, Paine House, exterior detail (photo: author)

43 H. H. Richardson, Paine House, living hall after 1989 restoration (photo: Richard Cheek)

Hunt's Grey Towers, the James Pinchot House at Milford, Pennsylvania (1884–86; fig. 44), demonstrates that Richardson had something else in mind. Here the towers, opened by windows with sandstone sills and heads but no jambs, join Olmsted's curvilinear terrace walls of the same stone to wed house to site in an inseparable bond, forming a clearly geological analogy. The Gurney House, of locally quarried stone, rides the crest of a granite ledge overlooking the seas as if it were a coastal outcropping.

Richardson's death at forty-seven meant that the accomplished works of his middle age became his definitive statements. There is no way of knowing what he would have achieved had he been given more time, but in just twenty short years he had managed to transform American architecture in

44 Richard M. Hunt, Grey Towers, the James Pinchot residence, Milford, Pa., 1884–86, exterior (photo courtesy Grey Towers, USDA Forest Service)

at least two important ways. In works like Trinity Church and the Allegheny County Courthouse he created seminal alternatives to the English Gothic and French classical buildings of his contemporaries and inspired a particularly American episode in the history of eclecticism known as the Richardsonian Romanesque. But even more important, in the Crane Memorial, the Old Colony Depot, the Marshall Field Wholesale Store, the Glessner and Potter houses, and the Ames Gate Lodge, he created in his own terms disciplined but fresh and diversified architectural forms for the American society of his day; and he left an individual if inchoate legacy rich in potential development for those who sought similar ends—in particular Louis Sullivan and Frank Lloyd Wright.

45 Louis Henry Sullivan (1856–1924) about 1895–1900 (© 1989 The Art Institute of Chicago. All rights reserved)

3

FORM FOLLOWS PRECEDENT

When Louis Sullivan (fig. 45) stepped off the transatlantic liner in New York harbor in May 1875, he was a mere eighteen years old. He had just spent ten months kicking around London, Paris, and Rome, with some time at the Ecole des Beaux-Arts, and was on his way to begin his career in architecture in Chicago, just then rebuilding after the great fire and destined to become the economic and cultural leader of the burgeoning Midwest. Although this precocious young man was certainly filled with vague ambition, he could not then have foreseen the exalted if chronically ill-defined place he was to achieve in the history of his profession. He carried with him off the boat educational baggage that was at best a jumble of confused ideas. Years later in his *Autobiography of an Idea* (1922–24), he would make it seem that he had all the right answers—or at least all the right questions— by the time he left Europe (and so devoted only a cursory summary to the rest of his life!); but it was to be a decade and a half before he was to achieve anything like an architectural statement of his program, and even then it was rather confusedly articulated.

Sullivan was born in Boston in 1856 and began his architectural training at the age of sixteen. He enrolled in the new school of architecture at the Massachusetts Institute of Technology (MIT), then in Back Bay in a red brick, classical building designed a decade earlier by William G. Preston. His jump from Boston's English High School to MIT after just two years was to set a pattern for his formal education: he was a youngster impatient with the impersonal drudgery of the classroom. He entered MIT in October 1872 and left at the end of the academic year. There he encountered a transplanted educational system based on, and in part taught by a recent *diplomé* of, the Parisian Ecole. And that meant, of course, intense study of classicism and specifically of the vocabulary of the orders based on Italian masters such as Vignola. The late *Autobiography* tells us that Sullivan thought of this architecture as dead, in contrast to the tower of the new Brattle Square Church a few steps away, a work "conceived and brought to light by the mighty Richardson, undoubtedly for Louis's special delight." And, he was to write, he gradually realized that the program at MIT was a "pale reflection" of the method of the Ecole des Beaux-Arts itself. He decided to move on to the source in Paris.

After a summer in Philadelphia (a brief but seminal moment to which we must shortly return) and a winter and spring in Chicago working for William Le Baron Jenney, an engineer turned architect who was to be called the father of the Chicago school of commercial architecture, the itinerant Sullivan, still in his seventeenth year, set sail for Paris in July 1874. He entered the Ecole in the fall, just nine years after Richardson had left it. Although he tells us almost nothing about his experience in the Atelier Vaudremer, he certainly encountered in this conservative institution much the same training as his older compatriot had. Sullivan later verbally abused classicism and the Ecole, but his works show that he remained ambivalent about their worth. Although he was later to deny vociferously the overt trappings of classical style he encountered in Paris, as he had at MIT, the *parti* of his most famous commercial works, the Wainwright and Guaranty buildings (see figs. 61 and 63), is based upon the classical schema. In addition, his later quick sketches, such as the orthogonal notation for the Eliel apartment building project of 1894 (fig. 46), certainly owe something to Ecole design procedure beginning with the *esquisse;* and the French method of rationally organizing a building program seems weakly reflected in his mature and superficially lucid statement of purpose, his 1896 essay "The Tall Office Building Artistically Considered."

Unlike Richardson, who studied and worked in Paris for more than six years and thus made its message a fundamental part of his medium, Sullivan must have barely touched base at the Ecole in the few months he attended (during which he also journeyed to Rome). He later wrote that he came away thinking "headquarters" no more cogent to his needs than its "pale reflection" in Boston's Back Bay. No drawings for Ecole projects survive from his hand. What do exist from this period are a pair of sheets containing rather prosaic studies of the Tuscan and Doric orders after Vignola (if indeed these do not date from his stay at MIT) and several others that reflect the very different experience he had in Philadelphia in the summer after leaving MIT (see fig. 49). Classrooms and ateliers were not places where Sullivan could learn; he absorbed by direct interaction with individuals he admired.

During that earlier summer in Philadelphia Sullivan had encountered an architect, a method of ornamental design, and a commercial architecture that were to have profound impact on his subsequent development. The man was Frank Furness, who in June 1873 with his first partner, George Hewitt, was designing a number of picturesque buildings, including that for the now demolished Guarantee Trust and Safe Deposit Company on Chestnut Street (1873–75), and overseeing construction of his first major work,

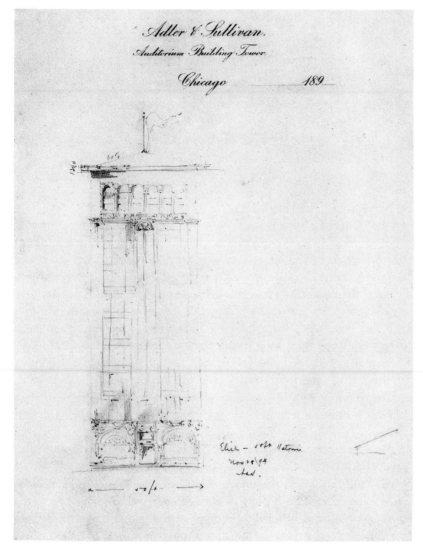

46 Louis H. Sullivan, Eliel Apartment project, 1894, preliminary sketch (Avery Architectural and Fine Arts Library, Columbia University in the City of New York)

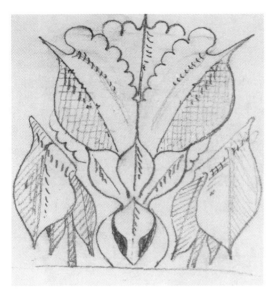

47 Frank Furness, sketch for floral ornament, undated (private collection; photo courtesy George E. Thomas)

the Pennsylvania Academy of the Fine Arts (figs. 6 and 48). As we have seen, the latter is a paradigm of creative eclecticism combining primarily French and English sources. Fifty years later Sullivan, in the only information we have about this episode, recalled with contempt the eclecticism of the office, assigning the use of sources to Hewitt, "a man who kept his nose in books." Remembering Furness as being at odds with the educational aims of the school at MIT, he thought of him as someone who "made buildings out of his head" and recalled his admiration for Furness's extraordinary freehand draftsmanship. And it was probably in Furness's drawings, especially his drawings for floral decoration, that Sullivan found a beginning direction for his own extraordinary ornamental talent (to say nothing of his interest in caricature, a droll sport in which Furness fully indulged).

In 1873 Furness's ornamental style was closely dependent on design theories originating in both England and France. In publications of the third quarter of the century by Owen Jones (*The Grammar of Ornament*, 1856), Christopher Dresser (*Principles of Decorative Design*, 1873), V.-M.-C. Ruprich-Robert (*Flore ornementale*, 1866–76), and even E. E. Viollet-le-Duc (among others, the *Entretiens sur l'architecture*, 1863 and 1872), ornamental patterns were rooted in nature, but the study of the history of design had led these theorists to develop rules for the use of natural form that drew upon a mathematical conception of nature as old as Plato. In the words of Jones's *Grammar*, for example, "flowers or other natural objects

48 Furness and Hewitt, Pennsylvania Academy of the Fine Arts, exterior detail, ca. 1873 (photo: author)

should not be used as ornaments, but conventional representations founded upon them," and "all ornament should be based upon geometrical construction." In other words, the ornamentalist was to study natural form as the basis for conventionalized patterns derived from their geometric organization. To use John Ruskin's terms in *The Seven Lamps* (for even this champion of the exact imitation of nature in art also recommended the process), the designer "gathered" in nature then "governed" its patterns by constructing geometric analogues to them. The process transcended national stylistic boundaries, and it was to have an important impact upon twentieth-century design as the first step toward abstraction.

In a brief article on "Hints to Designers" published in *Lippincott's Magazine* in May 1878, Furness advised prospective draftsmen to work "directly from life or Nature. . . . There is nothing in Nature—plant, bird, beast or fish—that cannot be brought into play as either the main feature or an accessory in a design." His surviving sketchbooks demonstrate his method of developing ornamental detail from nature. Drawings of plain and exotic plantlife, animals, and even humans vie with architectural studies. There are drawings, for example, of a turk's cap lily shown in views akin to an architect's orthogonal projections, that is, as if in plan and elevation. Furness found this way of recording nature in the publications of Jones, Ruprich-Robert, and others. By so drawing a flower (or a mouse or a frog) the draftsman "gathers" information about its axially generated forms. In other sketches the "governing" process is complete, and forms obviously derived from nature are transformed into balanced, axial, conventionalized patterns. Page after page is devoted to these stiff conventionalizations of flora (fig. 47) and fauna. These drawings then become the models for carved, cut, cast, stenciled, incised, wrought, or other decorative patterns used in buildings from Paris to London to Philadelphia. The conventionalized floral patterns on the Pennsylvania Academy building found in the tympana above the windows flanking the central *pavillon* of the Broad Street front are perfect examples (fig. 48), as were the ornamental entrance door panels of the Guarantee Trust. In both the stem typically forms a vertical central axis to right and left of which the simplified leaves are presented in frontal balance. Similar patterns are found throughout these and other contemporary works by Furness and his firm. Sullivan may have been a student of nature from early childhood, as he emphasizes in his *Autobiography*, and at least one drawing from 1875 records him dissecting a lotus in pursuit of its structure; but he first learned how to transform nature into ornament in Furness's drafting room.

Drawings for those Pennsylvania Academy or Guarantee Trust floral patterns might well have been on the boards in Furness's office when Sullivan drafted there during the summer and early fall of 1873. If they were not, there were certainly others of the same character. In any event, it was most likely through Furness that Sullivan learned of English and French theories of conventional ornamental design, and it was probably in Furness's office that he first began to develop the decorative drawing that was to become one of his major accomplishments. The drawings from his hand that survive from his Parisian days reflect his experience with Furness. They are either tracings of ornament after Ruprich-Robert, or they are patterns for fresco decoration that in some instances are close cousins of Furness's drawings for architectural ornament and in all instances were derived from European theories of conventionalization filtered through Furness's practice (fig. 49). And just as Furness instructed Sullivan in the art of conventionalization, so Sullivan was to pass the method on to his protege,

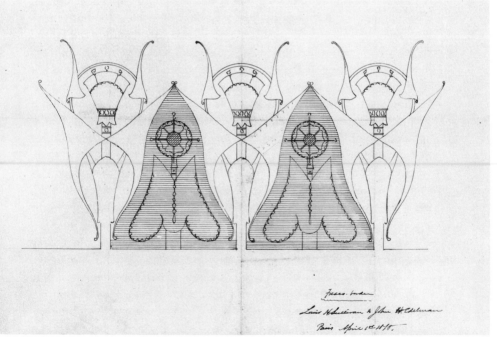

49 Louis H. Sullivan, sketch for floral ornament, 1875 (Avery Architectural and Fine Arts Library, Columbia University in the City of New York)

Frank Lloyd Wright. Sullivan was to develop the system into his own personal ornamental style (see fig. 51); as we shall see, Wright was to use it as a basis for his theory of organic architecture in which entire structures could be conceived as geometrical analogues of nature (see figs. 98–99).

The buildings and ornament of Frank Furness were not the only aspects of the Philadelphia professional scene that seem to have attracted the young Sullivan in the summer of 1873. During the middle of the century the architects of Philadelphia, like their Boston colleagues, had developed a distinctly local commercial style. In Boston it was the stringent, horizontal stone block that characterized the work (and so influenced Richardson); in Philadelphia, with its narrow street-front building lots, it was the pinched, vertical facade organized into continuous piers embracing several floors marked by recessed spandrels and often capped by an arcade. A few steps away from Furness's office near Third and Chestnut streets stood a thick cluster of these buildings. The best known, now demolished, is William Johnston's Jayne Building of 1849, its central block rising eight stories plus two-story tower. The Chestnut Street facade was of Venetian Gothic design, with attenuated granite colonnettes rising above a ground-floor base to crowning circular openings perched atop pointed arches. The horizontals were recessed and the voids infilled with glazing. Stephen Button's Leland Building of 1855, around the corner on Third Street and still standing, exhibits a limited classical decorative vocabulary on a narrow, five-story facade of diminishing ceiling heights. This built-in "perspective" emphasizes the building's verticality. Recessed spandrels emphasize the continuous Quincy granite piers rising above the ground floor to terminate in semicircular arches (fig. 50). The plan incorporates an interior light court. Any number of other preserved and demolished examples of the type could be cited. Nearly everyone who has recently written on Sullivan has recognized that this vertical emphasis stuck with him and reemerged in some of the tall office buildings of the 1890s on which his reputation principally rests (see fig. 61).

Those drawings for fresco designs produced by Sullivan in France during the winter of 1874–75 (see fig. 49) form a link between Paris, Philadelphia, and Chicago. Sullivan had worked in the latter city before going on to the Ecole, and he returned there to decorate interiors of religious buildings designed by his friend from his former stay, John Edelmann. One of the Parisian sketches bears Edelmann's name as well as Sullivan's, so while a student in Paris he was practicing Furnessic conventionalized ornamental design for commissions in Chicago. It would seem that his Ecole experience was

50 Stephen D. Button, Leland Building, Philadelphia, 1855, exterior (photo: author)

51 Louis H. Sullivan, sketch for floral ornament, 1885 (Avery Architectural and Fine Arts Library, Columbia University in the City of New York)

merely one part of his effective development. By the time he boarded the ship for his return to the United States, he had in just two and a half years of alternating classroom and practical experience learned enough to know what he liked and what he did not like. The way ahead was certainly not clear, but the path just traveled had made some choices more desirable than others. He probably sensed that the "dead" classical authority of MIT and the Ecole was insufficient to his aims. As he put it in the late *Autobiography*, he had "wished to be impelled by the power of the living." He was eventually to find that only Richardson, "sole giant of his day" among American architects, had sought and achieved the same individual vitality.

Through John Edelmann, Sullivan eventually joined Dankmar Adler, first as helper and eventually as partner, in the Chicago firm of Adler and Sullivan (the name first appears as such in 1883). Adler was an established architect some twelve years Sullivan's senior. He brought to the firm clients, engineering skills, and stability, all assets that complemented Sullivan's strengths and balanced his weaknesses. The partnership lasted until the middle of the next decade and rose to become one of the leading architectural firms in the Midwest. It was during his years as Adler's partner that Sullivan came into possession of his full powers; it was soon after Adler's departure that those powers began to fail. However else we assess the older man's contribution to the success of the firm, it was he who provided the framework within which Sullivan flowered.

That flowering occurred late in the 1880s, however, and in a series of earlier projects Sullivan had first to work his way through the vagaries of picturesque design and an overdependence on Philadelphian example in both buildings and their ornament. For a host of early Chicago works, such as the Max Rothschild Building of 1880 to 1881, the Revell Building of 1881 to 1882, and the Martin Ryerson and A. F. Troescher buildings of 1884 (fig. 52), Sullivan developed variations on the conventionalized natural ornament he had learned in Philadelphia. Surviving details in glazed terra-cotta from the J. M. Scoville Factory (1884–85) are clearly evolved from a starting point in Furness's Pennsylvania Academy decoration. His ornamental drawing dated late September 1885 displays his personal graphite touch while it clearly derives from the characteristic pattern of axial stem and symmetrical leafage he found in Furness's decorative work and its sources (fig. 51). But around the middle of the decade he also began to recall occasionally that other Philadelphia image, the vertically articulated commercial facade, in works such as the Knisely building of 1884 or the Scoville, and the Selz, Schwab factories of 1887. In the Troescher Building he combined Furnessic ornament with a modified (and neutralized) Philadelphia pier system infilled with glass, to create his own prototype for some of his commercial work of the next decade.

In other designs from these first ten years, however, Sullivan proved himself to be more generally a man of his time, swinging between the extremes of Anglo-eclectic picturesqueness, in works such as the Zion Temple of 1885 or the Kohn, Adler, and Felsenthal residences of the same year (fig. 53), and the Franco-classical crispness of the néo-Grec, as in a group of three connected flats for Max Rothschild of about 1883 (fig. 54). As Richardson had in the period between 1866 and 1872, so Sullivan bent to the prevailing and contradictory winds of transatlantic fashion in the period between 1876 and 1886.

Until the mid-1880s Sullivan more or less ran with the crowd. During the second half of the decade, however, he had perhaps read enough of Emerson, and certainly enough of Whitman, to agree with the sentiment expressed in "Self-Reliance" that "whoso would be a man, must be a nonconformist," and in *The Leaves of Grass* that "works made here in the spirit of other lands, are so much poison in the States." In 1887, having discovered Whitman's celebration of "self and nation" (to borrow Justin Kaplan's apt characterization), he wrote to the poet that he, too, was "reaching for the basis of a virile and indigenous art." And as it happened, it was to the virile mature works of Emerson's Massachusetts neighbor, H. H. Richardson, works that seemed to respond with vitality to the call for a cultural nationalism, that Sullivan turned for guidance. Here was precedent that was living rather than dead. Although the elder Sullivan tried to present himself as "a man outside of history" (in the words of David Andrew), neither he nor anyone else can escape the conditions created by date and place of birth. When he needed vivid forms to fulfill his clients' needs, he found those of Richardson useful models, and he thus assumed a historical relationship with his recently deceased precursor.

Near the end of his life, as we have seen, Sullivan recalled the "fairy tale" tower of Richardson's Brattle Square church as a "special delight," in contrast to what he then called the dead language of Italian and French classicism he encountered at MIT in the early 1870s; and we may imagine that in Chicago in the late 1870s and early 1880s he kept abreast of the older architect's much-publicized work. Although in 1903 he wrote that he doubted that Richardson had had much influence upon his "mental growth," the older architect did have a demonstrable impact upon his maturation as a designer. Richardson's unexpected and nationally reported

52 Adler and Sullivan, Troescher Building, 1884, exterior (photo: courtesy of the Richard Nickel Committee)

death in April 1886, the local unveiling of his last commercial masterpiece, the Marshall Field Wholesale Store, in June 1887, and the publication of Van Rensselaer's handsome and unprecedented *Henry Hobson Richardson and His Works* in May 1888 (one of three publications in Sullivan's library devoted specifically to Richardson and his work), all served to focus atten-

53 Adler and Sullivan, Kohn, Adler, and Felsenthal houses, Chicago, 1885, exterior (from Morrison, *Sullivan*, 1935)

tion on the man and his achievement at the very moment Sullivan was engaged with Adler in creating the cornerstone of his fame, the Auditorium Building. It was Sullivan's adaptation of Richardsonian quietude and massiveness that established that work as his first major accomplishment.

The clearest statement of the impact the Field store (see fig. 26) had on Sullivan, as we have seen, is found in the "Oasis" chapter of the "Kindergarten Chats." Of the Field store Sullivan said in effect what Whitman had said of his own major work: "who touches this touches a man." Here, Sullivan wrote, is "a male; for it sings the song of procreant power, as the

54 Adler and Sullivan, Rothschild flats, Chicago, 1883, exterior (from Morrison, *Sullivan*, 1935)

others have squealed of miscegenation." Here, he wrote, "stone and mortar
. . . spring into life"; here was a "rich somber chord of manliness"; here
he "would place a modest wreath upon the monument of him who stood
alone, an august figure in his art"; here, he agreed with his pupil, was a
structure "simple, dignified and massive." These and other phrases from
the "Oasis" suggest that Sullivan read Richardson the man as he read Richardson's building. As Phillips Brooks had said in his eulogy to the older
architect, "the man and his work are absolutely one," and both were excep-
tional within the context of the architectural profession of the day. Richard-

55 Adler and Sullivan, Auditorium Building, Chicago, 1886–89 exterior (photo: Cervin
Robinson)

son was an Emersonian individualist, a Whitmanesque force, the example of whose inchoate works suggested a direction for Sullivan to follow, creatively, without the mimicry of the Richardsonians.

When Sullivan realized what Richardson had achieved at the Field store, like the Auditorium a massive building occupying a full half-block, he altered his early designs for the Auditorium, editing out picturesque accretions in efflorescent terra-cotta to achieve a disciplined and integrated stone block broken only by the squared-off tower (fig. 55). He took over Richardson's powerful, low-sprung semicircular arches, the pattern of articulation of the Field facades, and the use of rock-faced horizontal ashlar, at least on the lower stories. These were all large, simple, tectonic devices for organizing and articulating a building. They were a far cry from the accumulations of features and ornament that marked his earlier work, including his earlier sketches for this building, and that of most of his contemporaries. He was to characterize the Field store in "The Oasis" as a place of calm amid a "host of stage-struck-wobbling mockeries," and he attempted to achieve the same effect in his Auditorium.

Which is not to say that he added nothing of himself to the Richardsonian mix. The openings of the main arcades at the Field store were voids neatly omitted from the constructional rock-faced stonework. Those of the main arcades of the Auditorium turn hesitantly into voids from the smooth-faced stonework of the wall through a series of receding archivolts. Sullivan is groping here; his handling of this detail lacks the conviction that characterizes Richardson's finest works. We reach the same conclusion by comparing Richardson's signature arches with those Sullivan used to open the ground floor of the Congress Street elevation. These are low and massive, made of large voussoirs (with keystones and adjacent stones emphasized) and surrounded by big rock-faced stone blocks (fig. 56); but the characteristic arch by the mature Richardson is made of gigantic voussoirs of identical magnitude and surrounded by huge masonry blocks (see fig. 16). There is a vast difference in coherence and scale between the one and the other. Although Sullivan is clearly learning from Richardson's example to work large rather than small, to think in unified wholes rather than in conflicting parts, he is just as clearly trying to adapt rather than copy the lessons of the older man. His ego precluded for him the role of epigone.

The plan, internal organization, and structural innovations of the Auditorium owe at least as much to Adler as to Sullivan. The ventilating system was of a widespread type Richardson used in the Allegheny County Courthouse (itself suggested by that at Parliament House in London, which Adler

56 Adler and Sullivan, Auditorium, exterior detail (from Szarkowski, *The Idea of Louis Sullivan*, 1956)

57 Adler and Sullivan, Auditorium, dining room (after *Architectural Record*, 1892)

might have known). The profuse interior ornament is Sullivan's with the assistance of the newly arrived Wright, among others. The cultural center of the building, the auditorium proper, is wrapped in an outer, commercial shell, with a hotel occupying the wing facing Michigan Avenue and running down Congress Street to the tower, and a stack of offices occupying the Wabash Avenue side and the tower. Adler's acoustical design made the great room then one of the best for music in the country; Sullivan's ornamental embellishment made it one of the visually richest rooms of the era. Within the hotel, the lobby, bar, and main dining room (a Richardsonian barrel-vaulted space; fig. 57) especially received the decorator's lavish attention as well. By this time, Sullivan's ornament had developed from the stiffly constructed, angular patterns of Furness toward the continuously curvilinear forms, perhaps derived in part from Viollet-le-Duc, in which the underlying geometric structure is overlaid by more animated and more luxuriant

87

58 Adler and Sullivan, Kehilath Anshe Ma'ariv Synagogue, Chicago, 1889–91, exterior
(photo: Chicago Historical Society)

foliage. Wright was to call this Sullivan's "efflorescence." It was probably as
Sullivan worked on the drawings for this decoration that Wright joined
him; there are preserved fragments of rejected sketches for this ornament
that are attributed to the young draftsman. At the Auditorium, then, Sullivan's emerging decorative genius, Wright's emerging career, and the late
Richardson's living example came together with Adler's structural skills to
create a major American building. Its success led to a series of commercial
commissions upon which the reputation of the firm of Adler and Sullivan,
and especially of its principal designer, chiefly rests.

In *Genius and the Mobocracy* Wright recalled that Sullivan one day
threw a penciled elevation on his drafting board with the comment that it
was the "last word" in Romanesque. The building was the Walker Warehouse in Chicago, so the year must have been 1888. That smooth-faced,
round-arched block was, after the Auditorium, the outstanding work
erected during Sullivan's earliest Richardsonian phase, an episode that included the design of clubs and residences, religious and commercial work.
Although Sullivan employed Richardson's characteristic forms, what he
must most have admired in the older man was his break with contemporary

fashion: his imposition of order onto the picturesque and his search for a language of form that would suggest an Emersonian or Whitmanesque independence from overtly foreign ideas. Other than the Auditorium and the Walker Warehouse, few of Sullivan's Richardsonian works from this era are among his happiest buildings. The exterior of the Kehilath Anshe Ma'ariv Synagogue in Chicago (1889–91; fig. 58), for instance, is a bland, reductive stone block with Richardsonian arches. A stale, reiterative work, it would fall into oblivion did it not contain an interior noted for its acoustics and bear Sullivan's name as designer. Such works represent an episode of experimentation with a manner that, like that of Furness, was ultimately foreign to Sullivan's aims. While Sullivan admired and learned from Richardson's unhesitantly bold statements, the ponderous vocabulary in which they were expressed was created for a pre-skeletal structural era, an era that effectively drew to a close as Sullivan worked on the Auditorium Building and the Walker Warehouse.

American commercial architecture was dramatically altered in the second half of the 1880s with culminating developments in Chicago in the fireproofed steel structural armature or skeleton. The metal frame opened the wall and liberated the building from the ground. It generated light skeletal masses infilled with glazing. It called for an architectural articulation different from the heavy, load-bearing masonry structures of the preindustrial centuries that had sustained Richardson's aims. The transformation in urban office buildings is made clear in Chicago by a comparison between Burnham and Root's Monadnock Building of the mid-1880s and their Reliance Building of 1890. The former is a traditional, solid, load-bearing, broad-based masonry block (fig. 59); the latter, a delicate, glazed, lightweight lantern employing the latest in structural methodology (fig. 60; also see fig. 29). The one represented the past, the other, the future of tall-building technology and appearance. Once the metal frame was in common use, Sullivan could learn nothing about its expression from the precedent works of Richardson (with the exception, perhaps, of the maverick Ames Store of 1886; see fig. 31); and in fact his continued use of the Richardsonian arch, a traditional loadbearing masonry form, in skeletal design confused his search for a clear architectural expression of current commercial purpose. Yet Richardson's last buildings suggested to Sullivan a way of reducing overall forms to their most visually economical packages. Sullivan was to articulate that package in a variety of ways, including vertical accents recalled from Philadelphia, and to ornament it with accents developed out of the tradition of conventionalized decoration he had encountered in Fur-

59 Burnham and Root, Monadnock Building, Chicago, 1885–92, exterior (photo: courtesy of the Richard Nickel Committee)

60 Burnham and Root, Reliance Building, Chicago, 1890, 1894–95, exterior (photo: Chicago Historical Society)

ness's office. In designing his most important works from the Wainwright Building in St. Louis to the Schlesinger & Mayer Store in Chicago, Sullivan drew upon the living lessons of Richardson, Furness, Philadelphia, and his Chicago peers, while he also on occasion drew upon the classical vocabulary of MIT and the Ecole. In the urban commercial building of the 1890s, as we shall see in the next chapter, out of these precedents he struggled to create an individual architectural statement.

4

THE TALL OFFICE BUILDING
INCONSISTENTLY CONSIDERED

Louis Sullivan's primary reputation rests on his designs for a series of commercial buildings erected during the 1890s in Chicago, St. Louis, Buffalo, and New York City. Although he and his firm turned out other building types as well, it is to the tall office building that his name is firmly attached. He is thus a major figure in the development of urban American architecture subsequent to Richardson's work at the Marshall Field Wholesale Store (fig. 26). Sullivan was to design some fine individual buildings, but as a group they exhibit a lack of consistency that stems from his inability to conceive and articulate his aims clearly. The fact that Sullivan's achievement cannot be simply defined derives from his ambiguity of purpose. Although it goes against the mass of scholarship devoted to finding a consistency in Sullivan's work, there is another reading of his buildings and his writings that points up his inconsistencies.

Sullivan's design for the building he considered his first mature work, the Wainwright in St. Louis (fig. 61–62; see fig. 64), stems from his years under the primary influence of Richardson, and it would come as a surprise if there were no traces of this immersion on the building. The first version, published, to be sure, over the name of local architect Charles K. Ramsey and therefore perhaps predating Sullivan's intervention, was a round-arched derivation from the Field store. As built, the Wainwright shared with the Field store the external appearance of a solid and coherent block. It was thus unlike the layered and ornamental richness of contemporary "Richardsonian picturesque" commercial buildings such as Burnham and Root's Woman's Temple in Chicago (1890–92) or George B. Post's Erie County Savings Bank in Buffalo (1890–93; see fig. 69), or the undulating glazed towers of Holabird and Roche's Tacoma Building (1887–89) or Burnham and Root's Reliance Building in Chicago (see fig. 60). Yet, again, as with the Field store, the block was deeply eroded by a necessary light court, and like the Field (and most other commercial blocks of the day), the design of its principal

61 Adler and Sullivan, Wainwright Building, St. Louis, 1890–91, detail of exterior (photo: Jean Baer O'Gorman)

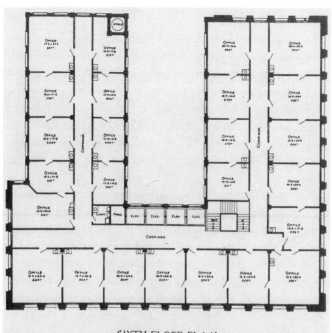

SIXTH FLOOR PLAN

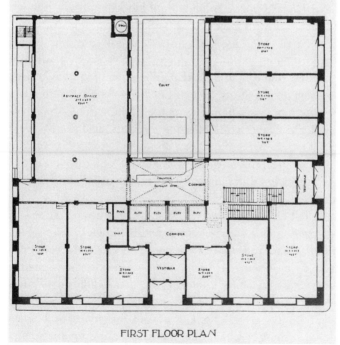

FIRST FLOOR PLAN

62 Adler and Sullivan, Wainwright, plan (from Morrison, *Sullivan*, 1935)

facades was abandoned in the walls of that court. Sullivan seems to have learned from Richardson to adapt the regular pattern of segmentally arched fenestration in a brick wall from the older industrial buildings of New England, although there were other Chicago structures that seemed to exhibit this same influence, most notably Burnham and Root's Montauk Block (1881–82). Yet, by the time he threw the drawing for the Wainwright facade on Wright's desk—an *esquisse* he later said took him three minutes, clearly an Ecole-inspired procedure—he was designing for a skeletal frame; and the example of Richardson's work could apply only in very general terms, as Sullivan apparently sought appropriate expression for a building program and a structural technology the older architect never faced. Does this lack of precedent in some measure account for the way Sullivan floundered in his search for a consonant articulation of the new architectural problem?

In March 1896 *Lippincott's Magazine* carried an article by Sullivan on "The Tall Office Building Artistically Considered," in which he tired to detail the practical and the poetic aspects of skyscraper design. It applied most directly to the Wainwright's "sister," as the architect called it, the recent Guaranty Building in Buffalo (1894–96; fig. 63; also see fig. 70), but it related to other of Sullivan's commercial blocks as well. Although this is probably the most lucid piece he ever wrote (Wright's unkind characterization of Sullivan's 1886 "Essay on Inspiration" as so much "baying at the moon" unfortunately all too accurately describes much of what he wrote about building), and contains a ringing statement of that (by others) mindlessly repeated phrase "form follows function," Sullivan in this article—as in the Wainwright, the Guaranty, and other commercial structures—failed to achieve a clear integration of space, structure, and exterior expression. Nowhere in this contemporary piece do we find an explicit prescription for "a realistic architecture based on well-defined utilitarian needs" that the architect, writing his *Autobiography* in the early 1920s, said he was looking for at the height of his career.

In "The Tall Office Building" Sullivan began with the rational approach to problem analysis he had encountered at the Ecole. Like a student, he did not question what lay behind the program as given, the social conditions that resulted "in a demand for the erection of tall office buildings." The conditions were, in his brief catalogue, the facts that businesses needed offices, elevators made vertical travel easy and comfortable, steel construction made great heights achievable, and urban congestion put a premium on land values. In more specific focus, these facts called for the erection of an urban building that would have, according to Sullivan's ordering: (1) a base-

63 Adler and Sullivan, Guaranty (Prudential) Building, Buffalo, 1894–96, exterior (photo: Cervin Robinson)

ment containing the power plant, (2) a ground floor devoted to retail shopping, (3) a second floor that was largely an extension of the first, (4) tier upon tier of identical office cells, (5) an attic story which contained the upper terminals and returns of the mechanical system, and a common entrance (that Sullivan mentioned the latter "finally, or at the beginning rather" seems to point up his disinterest in logical process). Each of these elements required its own external articulation, as in the floors of offices, which were to take their cue from the individual cell, or the common entrance, which must be placed and designed to attract the eye. Sullivan, of course, was concerned here only with the facade of his office building; he relegated structure, light courts, and elevator design and placement to the realm of the purely utilitarian. And designing for utility was the least of his concerns.

Having subjected his problem to prosaic analysis, Sullivan now returned to his real concern, the poetic realm: "We must now heed the imperative voice of emotion." It demanded that the chief characteristic of this building be identified, and here Sullivan apparently recalled the vertically articulated commercial blocks of mid-century Philadelphia (see fig. 50): the answer was loftiness. He then launched into that oft-quoted and stirring demand of the skyscraper that "It must be tall, every inch of it tall. . . . It must be every inch a proud and soaring thing, rising in sheer exaltation that from bottom to top it is a unit without a single dissenting line." Sullivan's stated concern was that the external, artistic expression of the tall office building should reflect its internal spatial divisions and declare itself "tall, every inch of it tall." The function that its form should follow was poetically visual rather than prosaically utilitarian.

For Sullivan, in this article, the proper, or artistic, articulation of the facade was the essential problem in the design of the tall office building. The principal facades of the Guaranty are composed of terra-cotta organized into a two-story base, ten stories of offices marked by continuous piers and recessed spandrels, and an ornamental attic topped by a projecting slab. The principle facades of the Wainwright (fig. 61) are organized into a two-story base of smooth Missouri red granite, seven stories of offices marked by continuous brick piers and recessed ornamental terra-cotta spandrels stretching between broad corner piers, and an ornamental attic beneath a projecting cornice. According to Wright's much later account in *Genius and the Mobocracy*, when Sullivan showed him the pattern of the Wainwright facade, he recognized it as a breakthrough for the master, presumably a breakthrough from his current overtly Richardsonian work; but he also said he saw that facade as essentially unrelated to the structural system supporting it. "The frontal divisions were still artificial," he wrote. Sullivan "had conceived it as still a column. . . . Base, shaft, and capital were there with no direct or apparent relation to actual construction." (Despite this criticism, Wright was to ape Sullivan's solution in his design of about 1899 for the Abraham Lincoln Center in Chicago). Although the tripartite column was, in fact, among the prototypes for tall building design that Sullivan mentioned and rejected in his *Lippincott's* article, he did indeed emulate the classical column.

The facade, Sullivan wrote, should reflect his earlier analysis: "the outward expression . . . of the tall office building should in the very nature of things follow the functions of the building, and where the function does not change, the form is not to change." This program might work for the patterns of use within the building, but it neglects its structural armature, the lightweight gridwork of steel that permits its loftiness in the first place (fig. 64). Wright recognized this dichotomy in Sullivan's Wainwright facade; it applies to the Guaranty and other works as well.

In his analysis of the tall office building, Sullivan described the frame as "the true basis of the artistic development of the exterior" and then proceeded to ignore it in the rest of his article and, in significant ways, in the Wainwright and many other celebrated facades. It has been frequently remarked that the load carried by a corner pier in the structural frame does not require a broadened corner pier on the exterior; that the number of brick piers Sullivan used on the facades of both the Wainwright and the Guaranty is double the number of structural piers in the frame (nonbearing alternate piers begin above the level of ground-floor shop windows); that all piers read as if they rest upon a base composed of the first two stories, when in fact the structural piers begin at the level of the footings; and that the pier capitals in the Wainwright represent no actual structural function. The Richardsonian arches and arcades prominent in the least seven of Sullivan's most significant buildings and projects of the 1890s, such as the Union Trust Building in St. Louis (with C. K. Ramsey, 1892–93; fig. 65) and the Stock Exchange in Chicago (1893–94), to say nothing of the slender arcade recalling Philadelphia mid-century prototypes at the Guaranty, are completely foreign to the trabeated skeleton. Arcuated articulation is more appropriately found in load-bearing masonry structures such as the thirteen-story Ames Building in Boston by Richardson's successors, Shepley, Rutan and Coolidge (see fig. 32). All of this demonstrates a disjuncture between frame and facade that was to bother the mature Wright, who, by

64 Adler and Sullivan, Wainwright, in construction (*L'Architecture*, 1894: University of Pennsylvania Library; photo courtesy George E. Thomas)

65 Adler and Sullivan, Union Trust Building, St. Louis, 1892–93, exterior (photo: Emil Boehl, courtesy of the Missouri Historical Society)

the time he criticized the Wainwright system had evolved his own "organic" theory of design. And it suggests that even in his most characteristic work, Sullivan held in suspension conflicting ideas derived from the Ecole as well as Jenney, Richardson, and commercial mid-century Philadelphia. Nevertheless, Sullivan could conclude his *Lippincott's* article with an interminable sentence that suggests, inter alia, that an architect who designed such a building might "cease struggling and prattling handcuffed and vainglorious in the asylum of a foreign school" and create a living architecture "of the people, for the people, and by the people." As has been so often observed, Sullivan was a poet, not a logician.

The lack of logic that marks both the *Lippincott's* article and the Wainwright and Guaranty facades is endemic in Sullivan's work of the 1890s. He seems to have subscribed to Emerson's assertion in "Self-Reliance" that "with consistency a great soul has simply nothing to do." He left some twenty designs—projects and buildings—for tall commercial structures between 1890 and 1904. Since he accepted the social conditions that gave rise to the building type, his task, like that of all the designers of urban commercial buildings to follow, boiled down to developing a series of variations on how the skeletally supported block might be articulated. The lack of continuity between frame and facade in the Wainwright and Guaranty buildings is paralleled by the lack of consistency in the variety of his solutions. To avoid the use of identical structural and nonstructural "pierage" to obtain the expression of loftiness that marks the Wainwright and Guaranty, he adopted the medieval system of alternate pier widths in the Bayard Building in New York (1897–98; fig. 66), but any concern with the true expression of skeletal construction is belied by the retention of the arcade. In the Schlesinger & Mayer Store he abandoned loftiness as a goal altogether, eschewed the arch, and created a grid of continuous broad horizontals and discontinuous thin verticals that more nearly expresses the frame than any of his other formulations (fig. 67). In a design with Charles K. Ramsey for a thirteen-story office building in St. Louis (1897; fig. 68), however, he abandoned the expression of frame altogether in favor of regular tiers of squarish voids seemingly cut out from the planar brick walls. That the conflicting solutions at the Wainwright, the Schlesinger & Mayer, and other of Sullivan's experiments have all been indiscriminately heralded as "masterpieces" of early urban commercial articulation suggests that, in the end, it made little difference what system he chose.

If Sullivan found no way consistently to express artistically the tall office building during the decade of his ascendancy, what are we to make of his

66 Louis H. Sullivan, Bayard (Condict) Building, New York, 1897–98 (photo: Cervin Robinson)

late *Autobiography*? This is no usual autobiography, of course, but a chronicle of the young Sullivan's intellectual development as recounted by the old Sullivan, on the model of the *Education* of Henry Adams, as Sherman Paul noted long ago. It is discursive and often even tediously garrulous except where the author treats of his mental growth under the tutelage of various teachers, culminating with a Monsieur Clopet in Paris. This tutor in mathematics produced, according to Sullivan, demonstrations *"so broad as to admit of* NO EXCEPTION!!" (Sullivan's typography), an idea Sullivan thought could be applied to architecture as to geometry through the formula "form

67 Louis H. Sullivan, Schlesinger & Mayer Store (Carson Pirie Scott), Chicago, 1899–1904, exterior (photo: Chicago Historical Society)

68 Louis H. Sullivan and Charles K. Ramsey, project for office building, St. Louis, 1897, perspective (© 1989 The Art Institute of Chicago. All rights reserved)

follows function." Although the elder Sullivan would have his readers be-
lieve he had achieved his end, had succeeded in his search for "a true normal type" as he mentions in "The Tall Office Building," his *Autobiography*
scurries over his work in architecture, and for a very good reason. As we
have seen, he had not in fact achieved, either in his writings or his buildings, an inclusive solution to the articulation of the tall office building. His
achievement in his chosen field of design was partial and equivocal, and as
if in recognition of that fact, after 1904 (as we shall see) he retreated into
the familiar protection of Richardson's "lengthened shadow." In fact, he had
never entirely left it.

69 Buffalo, New York, about 1900, with Richard Upjohn's St. Paul's Cathedral, 1848–51,
Adler and Sullivan's Guaranty Building, 1894–96, and George B. Post's Erie County Savings
Bank, 1890–93 (by permission of the Buffalo and Erie County Historical Society)

If Sullivan's approach to articulation of the facades of his commercial blocks was (and is) not the primary determinant of his achievement in the realm of urban architecture, what was? We have noted that Sullivan learned nothing about the articulation of tall skeletal buildings from Richardson, but he did learn about individual urban scale and solid, quiet form from his Eastern predecessor (see fig. 30). Many of Sullivan's major works of the 1890s are distinguished from those of his contemporaries in Chicago and New York because they were solid, simply circumscribed, rectangular blocks, the facades of which, no matter how varied in pattern from one to the other, were internally coherently articulated. As we have seen, they were unlike the piled classical compositions of George B. Post or the glazed lanterns of Burnham and Root. Even more, they stood out dramatically amid the "stage-struck-wobbling mockeries" that constituted the urban matrix into which they were placed, "like meteors from another planet," to quote R. M. Schindler's 1920s characterization of Richardson's Field store. The same might be said of the impact of the Guaranty Building in Buffalo as it appeared amid its original neighbors by Richard Upjohn and George Post in a view made when it was new (fig. 69). Only by looking at Sullivan's commercial works in their original contexts can we understand how they, like the Field store, formed oases of visually economical form within the bristling, eclectic American city, for not only have their original contexts been completely transformed by ensuing development, but there seems little or no connection between Sullivan's solid blocks and the truly soaring and gleaming shafts of the twentieth-century city.

However we may assess Sullivan's contribution to the planning, mechanics, and engineering of the buildings of the firm of Adler and Sullivan, however confused we may find his program for the articulation of the tall office building, his forte was clearly as an ornamentalist. Here he could scarcely rely on Richardson for guidance. Ornament in Richardson's most personal works, usually derived from Romanesque or Byzantine sources, was an important but not an overtly conspicuous element of design. Richardson knew of the ornamental theories of his day—he owned copies of Owen Jones, Ruskin, and Viollet-le-Duc—but he never displayed a consistent, programmatic interest in the process of conventionalization except as it might generally account for his design of the Ames Monument in Wyoming (1879–82) and other examples of his geological analogy. As we have seen, Sullivan's ornament sprang not from Richardson but from other sources that initially reached him through Furness. However, where he got his ideas is only one question to ask. How he employed that ornament is another.

Sullivan's use of decoration was as inconsistent as his articulation of the tall building facade. At the beginning of his maturity, in the Auditorium and the Wainwright, he exhibited a relative clarity of decorative purpose that was to become confused in later work. He could have written of the Wainwright, as he did in 1891 of the Auditorium, that its "decorations are distinctly architectural in conception. They are everywhere kept subordinate to the . . . larger structural masses and subdivisions." The *parti* of the Wainwright is obviously a classical one, as we have seen, with two-story base, seven-story shaft, and one-story attic. It is in fact a rather broad and reassuringly stabile block with crisply planar base and corners, and sturdy, standing brick piers braced horizontally by ornamented spandrels (see fig. 61). The picturesquely animated terra-cotta panels are tightly controlled so that they reinforce the poetically tectonic diagram. The "main aperture or entrance" is picked out by a ribbon of geometric design, the portholes of the terminal attic are wreathed with lush vegetation, the standing piers end in capitals, and the interrupted spandrels exhibit at each level a different design derived from nature, some more conventionalized than others. The only false note is the applied ornament at the base of each pier. This inconsistent touch undermines the suggestion of stability that characterizes the rectangular, visual interplay of "structure" and "nature" elsewhere on the exterior, and it heralds more unfortunate characteristics in his later work. In the Wainwright, Sullivan's first and many would say finest facade pattern, there is a discipline that was perhaps a legacy of Richardson and that was certainly to loosen as other building designs came onto his drafting board.

Although the greater height, thinner corners, and visually more delicate piers at the later Guaranty Building in Buffalo more nearly suggest the light metal frame within, its classical analogies are also more overt than at the Wainwright, with columns at the base and doorways inspired by quattrocento Florence; and the all-encompassing filigree of geometric and foliate decoration begins to compromise the programmatic clarity of the earlier block (fig. 70). At the Schlesinger & Mayer Store (see fig. 67) the designer seemed once more to exercise architectonic control over his ornamental genius, for he concentrated his most lavish attention on eye-catching floral displays around ground-floor shop windows and the main entrance at State and Madison streets, while the openings in the grid above are edged by modest geometric jambs that underline the rectangular pattern of the frame beneath. Among Sullivan's surviving works, the Bayard Building (fig. 66), which combines medieval and classical motifs, represents the beginning of a decline. Here the lush leafage seems to overrun its fields, which, in any event, are no longer part of a "structural" interplay, as Sullivan like a jeweler created spotty and gaudy brooches seemingly pinned to a neutral ground. He was to repeat these devices in the Gage Building (1898–99) and elsewhere, as increasingly ornament took on a life of its own divorced from any tectonic pretext. The contrast between the Wainwright and these later works seems to exemplify Sullivan's own slanted distinction, expressed in an article published early in the decade, between integral and "stuck one" decoration: "in the former . . . there exists a peculiar sympathy between the ornament and the structure, which is absent in the latter," he wrote at the height of his powers. By the end of the decade those powers had markedly diminished.

Sullivan turned out his most characteristic and important, if increasingly less sure, works in the decade between the Wainwright Building and the

70 Adler and Sullivan, Guaranty Building, exterior detail (photo: Cervin Robinson)

Schlesinger & Mayer Store. For part of that time he was a partner in one of the major firms in America, and for all of it he was a leading architect of the second city in the country (and even erected a major work in the first). But by the end of that decade he had lost his right-hand man and his partner, and he had gradually begun that decline that was to drive him out of the Auditorium tower as the clients vanished from his door, leaving him destitute and alone by the time of his death. Despite the presence in Buffalo of his majestic and relatively new Guaranty Building, the Larkin commission

71 Louis H. Sullivan, National Farmers' Bank, Owatonna, Minn., 1906–8, exterior (photo: Cervin Robinson)

of 1902 went to Wright regardless of his lack of experience in commercial design.

After the Schlesinger & Mayer Store, Sullivan's work was largely confined to one church, a couple of houses, and a handful of small-town banks. For the architect of many major commercial buildings in Chicago, St. Louis, Buffalo, and New York City to find himself scratching for small work in Grinnell, Iowa, Owatonna, Minnesota, or Sidney, Ohio, seems a precipitous decline. Although these later buildings have drawn increasing attention and praise from critics and historians, in fact the work is uneven. Its chief historical interest, beyond its reflection of that decline, is in the resurgence of overtly Richardsonian imagery. It was as if Sullivan, again working at less than skyscraper scale, picked up where he had left off in the Kehilath Anshe Ma'ariv Synagogue of 1889 (see fig. 58). The best of the banks is the National Farmers' in Owatonna (1906–8; fig. 71), a work which, like the People's Savings and Loan in Sidney of a decade later, takes as its motif the broad Richardsonian arch Sullivan had first used in the Auditorium. The awkward People's Savings Bank of Cedar Rapids, Iowa (1911), on the other hand, seems a squat, trabeated variation on the earlier synagogue. Although these small, out-of-the-way buildings do contain some of Sullivan's most characteristic and breathtakingly beautiful ornament, they in fact represent the afterglow of a career whose sunset had occurred near the turn of the century.

Ultimately Sullivan's achievement lacks focus because he lacked a precision of purpose. His unstable personality was matched by his lack of intellectual clarity. He failed in the end to find that law that admitted of no exceptions, that law that was part of the idea he chased like a will-o'-the-wisp throughout a life that had risen to its apex in the Auditorium tower then plunged into an abyss of neglect and futility. But along the way he managed to combine the tradition of conventionalized ornament he encountered in Furness's office with a creative reading of Richardson's legacy; and through him flowed a continuity of achievement beginning with H. H. Richardson and ending with Frank Lloyd Wright. There seems no reason to revise Mumford's assessment in *The Brown Decades* that "Sullivan was the link between two greater masters."

72 Frank Lloyd Wright (1867–1959) about 1900 (photo courtesy the State Historical Society of Wisconsin)

5

A LONG FOREGROUND

When Frank Lloyd Wright (fig. 72) arrived in Chicago in the spring of 1887, he was about twenty years old, had just abandoned a brief career as student of engineering at the University of Wisconsin at Madison, and had decided to seek his future in the growing metropolis of the Midwest. Unlike Richardson or Sullivan at similar turning points, Wright had not and would never study in Europe, turning down, by his own later account, an offer to attend the Ecole des Beaux-Arts extended by the architect Daniel Burnham after the Columbian Exposition of 1893. Richardson was born in the South, thoroughly educated in New England and Paris, and eventually established a practice in the Boston area that was to spread to the Midwest. Sullivan was born in New England, was briefly educated in Boston and Paris, worked as briefly in Philadelphia, and practiced his profession largely in Chicago. Wright was born in 1867 in Wisconsin, eschewed Paris and all it stood for, and lived and practiced mainly in the Midwest throughout the period of concern to us here. The drift away from Eurocentric study and from the eastern shores to the inland sea witnessed in these successive biographies parallels the shift toward a cisatlantic architecture that marks the transformations through the works of these three men.

In later writings such as his *Autobiography*, Wright tried to create the impression that he arrived in Chicago as a fully formed architect ready to reshape the physical world misshapen by adherents of the Ecole and the picturesque. He, his followers, and some credulous historians have brought forth remarkably mature drawings showing Wright's fully formed ideas, which they date as early as 1887. There is no reason to accept this as any more than an aspect of Wright's characteristic rewriting of history, especially of his early history. Drawings certainly by Wright that can, as certainly, be dated to the first years of his work bear no resemblance to these backdated designs. As would have any other youngster fresh from the hinterland, however gifted, Wright arrived unformed as an architect, and it was to take him nearly a decade and a half to find his own manner. These years constituted the "long foreground" (a period Emerson assumed, in his famous letter to Whitman on the appearance of *Leaves of Grass* in 1855, had preceded "the beginning of a great career") to the unveiling of Wright's prairie house after 1900. He had much guidance along the way, especially (although obviously not exclusively) from those cicerones close at hand, the presence of L. H. Sullivan and the works of H. H. Richardson.

The influence of the Froebel kindergarten gifts on the development of Wright as a mature designer is a still moot aspect of his career, however frequently mentioned. Who is to prove that the somewhat mythical (and mystical) episode in his young life made any more impression upon the fledgling architect than his family's membership in the First Unitarian Church of Madison, a congregation housed in a Richardsonian Romanesque work of 1886 by Peabody and Stearns of Boston? What is more certain is that Wright's first works in Chicago, for Joseph Lyman Silsbee and indepen-

73 Frank Lloyd Wright, F. Ll. Wright House (right), 1889, and studio library (left), 1898, Oak Park, Ill., exterior (photo: Don Kalec, courtesy the Frank Lloyd Wright Home and Studio Foundation)

dently for his family in Wisconsin, established the direction of his career. Silsbee was an Eastern-born Chicago architect, who probably hired Wright because he had himself worked for Wright's family. He was a practitioner of the domestic shingle style, that picturesque wooden architecture ubiquitous along the coast and in the suburbs of the East. Although he had not "invented" it, Richardson had created some of the most disciplined and distinguished examples of the style in the Stoughton House in Cambridge, Massachusetts, and the Potter House in St. Louis (see fig. 37), and other designers east and west borrowed liberally from these as from all his works. From the beginning of his career, then, Wright was aware of Richardsonian style and associated with the domestic design that would remain the bulk of his work throughout a very long life.

By 1889, having established a household, Wright required a residence of his own, one he designed and built in suburban Oak Park west of the Loop. The Oak Park house culminated Wright's early, shingle style phase (fig. 73). The plan is hearth-centered, with the Richardsonian low-arched brick fireplace buried in an inglenook and the interior spaces extending to the outdoors through diamond-paned polygonal bays and an elevated piazza. The exterior front is dominated by a shingled equilateral triangle surrounding one simplified Palladian window. This exterior *parti* is a reduction of such well-known antecedents as the 1885 Chandler House by Bruce Price in Tuxedo Park, New York, a recently published work by a fashionable eastern architect of the high-priced, shingle-style "cottage" (although the Palladian motif within a gable could also be found on Richardson's Paine House [see fig. 41]). Silsbee had trained his apprentice well.

In 1898 Wright added to his Oak Park home a studio consisting of drafting room and offices, thus establishing an integration of family and work that recalled Richardson's arrangement. In Oak Park as in Brookline, "the life of the home and the life of the office went on together," as Van Rensselaer wrote of Richardson's setting. Architect, wife, children (coincidentally, six children in each case!), and draftsmen all took part in the hubbub of work and play. And Wright was to continue and expand upon this arrangement when he moved to Wisconsin in 1911.

Wright joined Adler and Sullivan probably in the late winter of 1887 to 1888 and quickly became Sullivan's right-hand man. He stayed until 1893. Sullivan took him on to help with drawings for the Auditorium Building, a work we have seen significantly indebted to Richardson's Field store, so Wright moved from an office suffused with Richardsonian domestic design to one concentrating on Richardson's latest commercial achievement. Sullivan was also at this moment reading deeply in the works of Walt Whitman, even writing to the poet about his own search for a "virile and indigenous art." None of this could have escaped such a bright and impressionable twenty-one year old. During Wright's stay in the Adler and Sullivan office, Sullivan had begun to search for an architectural expression of his own, in contrast to the borrowed European forms he had previously employed; and he had begun that search as a close student of the works of his distinguished predecessor. He undoubtedly shared these interests with his young drafts-man during late-night sessions in the Auditorium tower high above the city by the lake. Although Wright later lamented Sullivan's interest in Richardson and was to express ambivalence about Richardson's achievement throughout his life, there can be little question of Richardson's impact upon the young draftsman. When Sullivan undoubtedly pointed to works like the Field store as serene and living landmarks guiding the designer through the boiling seas of picturesque eclecticism, the young Wright must surely have listened and looked and learned.

It was reasonable that Sullivan would turn for inspiration to the Field store (see fig. 26), a mercantile block situated in an urban core, because he was himself about to embark upon a series of commercial structures in Chicago and elsewhere that would require a grasp of urban scale and economical form. The firm of Adler and Sullivan, however, was obliged to turn out other commissions as well, including residences, with which Sullivan had little patience. It was to Wright that these "lesser" works devolved, to the assistant designer who had had some experience with domestic architecture before joining the partners. Out of these years with Adler and Sullivan, Wright's largely unsought specialization in residential design developed, a speciality that was to last throughout his very long career. Although Wright wrote to Cudworth Beye at the time of his work on the Yahara River Boat House (1905), using words nearly identical to those Richardson reputedly spoke to J. J. Glessner and probably in general circulation among contemporary architects, that he would "desingn [sic] any thing for the W[isconsin] U[niversity] from a chicken house to a cathedral," in fact nonresidential work was to remain a small fraction of his output. Although during this period Wright designed buildings of major historical and aesthetic importance other than residences, most notably the Larkin Company Administration Building in Buffalo (1902–6) and Unity Church in Oak Park, Illinois (1904–7), the bulk of his achievement was in residential design. It was on this building type that he was to place his indelible mark.

Wright's earliest mark as an independent entity within the firm of Ad-

74 Frank Lloyd Wright for Adler and Sullivan, Victor Falkenau houses, Chicago, 1888, perspective (*Inland Architect*, 1888)

ler and Sullivan was his signature on a rendering of a row of three houses for Victor Falkenau published in the *Inland Architect* in June 1888 (fig. 74). He could not have been much more than a couple of months out of Silsbee's office. Assuming Wright was the designer of these unified facades as well as the delineator of this perspective, the Falkenau project stands in the same relationship to his development that the Auditorium (see fig. 55) stands to that of Sullivan, at least as regards its primary source of inspiration. For the design of his urban block Sullivan sought guidance in Richardson's Field store; for the design of the Falkenau houses Wright sought guidance in Richardson's other Chicago masterpiece, the recently completed John J. Glessner House.

The Glessner House (see figs. 33–35) stands on the south side of Chicago in an area certainly known to Wright because his employer lived in the neighborhood, and there were in the vicinity a cluster of residential commissions executed by the firm both before and after Wright joined it. It stands alone now, but to Sullivan and Wright it then stood out on Prairie

Avenue amidst a host of domestic "mockeries" such as Marshall Field's own mansarded Frenchman just down the street. As we have seen, the Glessner house was a domestic version of the Field store: a gray granite, horizontal ashlar fortress harboring a brick-walled garden within its courtyard. Given Sullivan's current focus on Richardson, he might have directed his drafts-man's attention to the Glessner as a suitable model of disciplined domestic design. Be that as it may, we can tell from the drawing of the Falkenau houses that Wright looked to the Glessner for his rock-faced, horizontal ashlar wall, his semicircular arches, his mullioned and transomed basement windows, and his trabeated upper openings divided by chubby columns. As with Sullivan's early projects for the Auditorium, the callow designer was reluctant to abandon entirely details such as the rounded second-story oriels more appropriate to the picturesque Queen Anne style. With the Fal-kenau facade Wright caught up with Sullivan in his study of the local archi-tecture of their East Coast predecessor. Each had picked a building appro-priate to his own concerns and through adaptation absorbed its lessons of quietude and massiveness.

Just as Sullivan saw the Field store against a backdrop of picturesque commercial "mockeries," so the young Wright through Sullivan's eyes mea-sured the Glessner against such domestic designs as Henry Ives Cobb's northshore "castle" for the Potter Palmers (1882; fig. 75). In an article pub-lished in the *Architectural Record* in March 1908, Wright wrote, in words picturesquely suited to his subject, of the domestic architecture of the 1880s that "the sky lines . . . were fantastic abortions, tortured by features that disrupted the distorted roof surfaces from which attenuated chimneys like lean fingers threatened the sky; the invariably tall interiors were cut up into box-like compartments, . . . and 'architecture' chiefly consisted in healing over the edges of the curious collection of holes that had to be cut in the walls for light and air and to permit the occupant to get in or out." Against such a bombastic backdrop the Glessner presented to Sullivan and Wright a welcomed serenity. As we shall see, however, Wright derived more from the Glessner than just its stern and quiet exterior.

Wright turned out a mixed assortment of residential projects from the time he joined Adler and Sullivan until the mid-1890s, a series of designs that show him ranging far and wide as he stumbled toward a look of his own. This period in the young Wright's career was akin to Richardson's apprenticeship from 1866 to 1872 and Sullivan's decade of searching be-tween 1876 and 1886. Although Wright was ultimately to return to Rich-ardson as his primary source, the designs of his apprenticeship days and

75 Henry Ives Cobb, Potter Palmer House, Chicago, 1882, exterior (photo: Chicago Historical Society)

later took him to such diverse fonts as the work of the French "revolutionary" eighteenth-century architect, Claude-Nicolas Ledoux, the *parti* of whose St. Germain house in Paris (1772) seems to join Sullivanesque ornament in the James Charnley House in Chicago (1891); the Dutch colonial, as in the gambrel-roofed and classically detailed Frederick Bagley House in Hinsdale, Illinois (1894), the English colonial, as in the Palladian-windowed Blossom House in Chicago (1892; fig. 76), a work akin to McKim, Mead and White's H. A. C. Taylor House in Newport (1885–86), and the Tudor, as in the original Nathan G. Moore house in Oak Park (1895). Yet even the Bagley House sports a Richardsonian eyebrow dormer, and the neoclassical Blossom house has a Richardsonian quietude about it. Moreover Wright here turned in part to the Glessner for the plan of the rectangular dining room extending into a semicircular bay (polygonal at the Glessner; see fig. 33), and the stairway, too, has a Richardsonian breadth. This mixed bag of residential designs represents the work of an architect exploring the myriad possibilities of his eclectic day. Because of his special historical position within the aura of Silsbee, Richardson, and Sullivan, however, Wright could at least by the time of his 1896 lecture to the University Guild of Evanston, Illinois, denounce the "Colonial and Renaissance, the chateau and the chalet." He could, that is, echo Emerson's query in "Self-Reliance": "why need we copy the Doric or the Gothic model?"

Wright left Adler and Sullivan in 1893; and in his later rewriting of his early history, he usually recognized the William Winslow House in River Forest, Illinois, of the same year as his "first" personal work (figs. 77–79). It is indeed an extraordinary and historically important design, for it represents Wright's first creative synthesis of the stimuli provided by Sullivan and, through Sullivan, Richardson. The house is set back on a flat suburban lot, its location fixed by an axis running perpendicular from the street along the entrance walk, through the front door, inglenook, masonry stack of back-to-back fireplaces, and rectangular dining room with semicircular extension, to dissipate in the rear yard. The public facade of the house itself (excluding the porte cochere) is implacably symmetrical, with the entrance flanked by square voids set into a limestone frame at the base of a slightly projecting two-story salient. Framed square voids in turn flank the central motif, and, with the central opening, are repeated at the second level. Each

76 Frank Lloyd Wright, George Blossom House, Chicago, 1892, exterior (from Hitchcock, *Nature of Materials*, 1942)

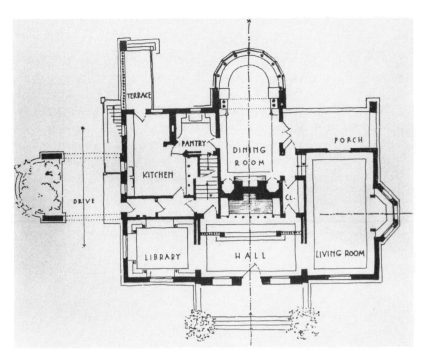

77 Frank Lloyd Wright, W. H. Winslow House, River Forest, Ill., 1893, plan (from Manson, *Wright*, 1958)

78 Frank Lloyd Wright, Winslow House, front (from Hitchcock, *Nature of Materials*, 1942)

story is treated differently. The ground floor is composed of closely laid, buff, Roman brick above the water table, while the second floor, set forward slightly from the plane below, is a frieze of dark ornamental stuccowork. Above the facade hovers a broad, originally orange tiled, hip roof the soffits of which are wide overhangs extending far beyond the plane of the wall. The hip is anchored by a low, central masonry chimney. The house presents a composed, formal face to the public beyond the clipped front law.

Around back all hell breaks loose (fig. 79). Here in the relative privacy of the rear yard, where the family unbuttons and relaxes, the rigid control of the facade gives way to picturesque clutter. The axis disappears: the massing is an informal asymmetrical melange of wings, porch, bay, stairtower, chimney, and dormer. This contrast between front and back is a dramatic architectural demonstration of the distinction between the public and private spheres of the domestic establishment; it is one of the characteristics that make the Winslow both a vivid experience and, as Norris Kelly Smith so insightfully observed, a cogent index to Wright's attitude toward the relationship between society and the nuclear family. It is also a creative reinterpretation of Richardson's design for the Glessner House.

The Sullivanesque elements in the Winslow are easily inventoried. The

79 Frank Lloyd Wright, Winslow House, rear (from Manson, *Wright*, 1958)

frame surrounding the entrance derives directly from Sullivan's design of 1891 for the Charlotte Wainwright tomb in St. Louis (we may ignore Wright's broad hints in *Genius and the Mobocracy* and elsewhere that it was he who designed this as well as other of Sullivan's best works, despite the fact that some working drawings for the tomb are in his hand). The decorative edge surrounding it, the ornamental frieze beneath the eaves, and the design and ornament of the delicate arcade before the inglenook beyond the entrance are Wrightian variations on Sullivanesque decorative motifs.

The Richardsonian character is more thoroughgoing. It is hinted at in details such as the low-sprung arches of the porte cochere (too thin to evoke Richardson's weight, however) and the square proportions of the openings of the front facade. It is formative in Wright's use of the tripartite layering of the frontal mass, piling frieze upon base and topping the whole with the hovering hip. This is the same horizontally stacked, disciplinary organization Richardson had developed for his libraries and depots. Its prototypes are especially evident in the photographic detail of the Ames Memorial Library (see fig. 17) or the drawing of the Woodland Station, both published by Van Rensselaer. But the Winslow dining room, like that of the earlier Blossom House, indicates that Wright had in mind a Richardsonian source closer to home. And indeed, the Glessner House is ultimately the prime inspiration for the most characteristic feature of the Winslow House, its differential characterization of public and private spheres. The Glessner was, in fact, a precedent manifesto of a cause Wright was only now beginning slowly to define.

Unlike the suburban Winslow, which is set back in isolation on its spacious plot, the urban Glessner pushes up against the public sidewalks at the intersection of two streets, but its forbidding granite exterior is even more austere than that of Wright's later house (cf. figs. 34 and 78). The Prairie Avenue facade that attracted Wright as early as 1888 is nearly as formal as is the main front of the Winslow: a central entrance is surrounded by axially balanced, regularly spaced rectangular openings. Symmetry is compromised here, however, by the driveway opening to the left and the windows above it, and this is a prime example, as we have mentioned, of Richardson's frequent counterplay between symmetry and asymmetry. But look again at the public face of the Winslow. If we now take into consideration all that we can see from the street, including the porte cochere to the left and the polygonal bay to the right, and remember the octagonal library originally intended to extend out to the right from the rear porch, we realize that Wright too has set up a symmetrical pattern and upset it with asymmetrical accretions.

These parallel compositional patterns on the external facades of the Glessner and the Winslow might seem coincidental if it were not for a second parallel that occurs around back (cf. figs. 35 and 79). The Glessner sets its formal shell against the public sphere so that it might better protect the informal walls and enclosed family courtyard reached by driving through the asymmetrically placed carriage entrance to the left of the Prairie Avenue facade. In the courtyard the stern granite exterior gives way to undulating brick walls with stone trim. Openings are larger and more plentiful, and the tall, rounded stairtower forms a picturesque foil to the squat, polygonal shape of the dining room bay. The interplay between bulging stairtower and dining room is an asymmetrically relaxed arrangement that Wright was to echo in the private rear of his Winslow House.

The Winslow House, with its Sullivanesque touches on a Richardsonian base, aptly represents Wright's relationship to the work of his predecessors at the beginning of his independent career. He had adapted Sullivan's ornamental accents, and he had absorbed Richardson's reposeful forms. From Sullivan at this point he had learned all he could, although as we shall see, he was to extend the uses of conventionalization beyond the merely decorative. From Richardson's example he had extracted the essential characteristics, but he was to return again and again during the next decade, and less

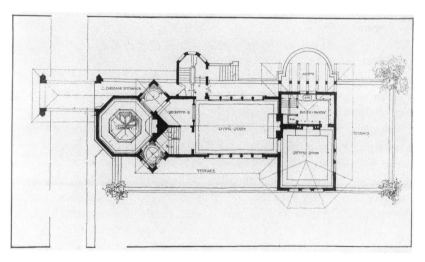

80 Frank Lloyd Wright, McAfee house project, 1894, plan (from Manson, *Wright*, 1958)

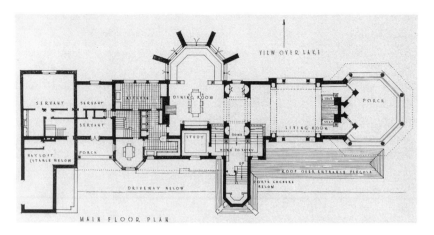

81 Frank Lloyd Wright, Joseph W. Husser House, Chicago, 1899, plan (from Manson, *Wright*, 1958)

frequently thereafter, to formal devices found in local works and in published plates. Eventually, since the works of Wright's maturity were to an extent adaptations and extensions, or transformations, of Richardson's example, the Richardsonian element was wholly absorbed into Wright's own manner.

The interrelationship among the works of Richardson, Sullivan, and Wright may be seen at its earliest and clearest in Wright's independent Winslow House, but it did not end there. Wright had nearly another decade of experimentation, of "foreground," before he arrived at the prairie house, his characteristically Midwestern, suburban domestic establishment (see fig. 87). In diverse residential commissions during this formative period he worked over Richardsonian ideas. Take, as examples, the McAfee House project intended for Kenilworth, Illinois (1894), and the Joseph Husser House (1899) that once stood in the Buena Park section of Chicago. Both had the layered, horizontal articulation and hovering roofs of the Richardsonian mass (the McAfee displayed Sullivanesque ornamental panels; the Husser sported a Sullivanesque frieze terminated by semicircular arcades), but it is in their plans that we find their true pedigrees.

In the plan of the McAfee project (fig. 80) there is a main axial alignment (interrupted, to be sure, by reception room, stairhall, and fireplace) of living room and octagonal library, with the projecting, polygonal stairtower set at right angles. In the Husser House plan (fig. 81) the main axis stretches in one direction through the inglenook and chimney stack onto an octagonal porch, while in the other direction it encounters offset cross axes, the one marking the projecting polygonal stairtower, as in the McAfee project, the other centering the dining room with polygonal extension projecting from the opposite side. These are but domestic adaptations of the plan of Richardson's Winn Memorial Library (see fig. 21), an equally unresolved project with main axis extending from library proper to octagonal museum and a polygonal stairtower protruding on a secondary cross axis. Richardson himself developed this arrangement of major and minor axes into a mature residential design in the Potter House (see fig. 36). There, rooms stretched along the main axis were opposed by an offset, cross-axial polygonal stairtower on the one side and dining room with semicircular extension on the other. Since the Potter plan seems not to have been published until recently, Wright perhaps did his own adapting from the Winn Memorial plan available in Van Rensselaer (or from the similar plan for the library at Burlington, Vermont). Not to forget Sullivan, he was to continue the line when, with his practice and his talents in decline after the turn of the century, he laid out the 1907 Henry Babson House in Riverside, Illinois, with many of the same relationships and the Richardsonian arch incorporated into the elevations. The embryonic cross-axial arrangement of the Husser House is an early glimmer of the fully developed cruciform plan of Wright's prairie house of the next decade (see fig. 89), so the impact of the older architect's mature work upon that of the younger is a direct one that includes planning processes as well as three-dimensional forms.

Once Wright had thoroughly learned the Richardsonian lesson, he could move on to other compatible sources of ideas; but once Richardsonian forms had become part of his design vocabulary, they continued to appear in his work more or less transformed for a number of years, even well beyond the introduction of his own prairie house in 1901. The asymmetrical combination of round arch and stubby tower of Richardson's Ames Gate Lodge or Crane Library reappears, reversed, in Wright's project for a barn for the Cooper House at LaGrange, Illinois, an undated (and consistently misdated) design that cannot be earlier than the late 1890s. The low, semicircular arch (of stone, brick, or shingle over frame) occurs frequently as both interior features such as fireplaces and exterior openings, as in the Lake Monona Boat House project (1893), the Devin House project of the mid-1890s, the Francisco Terrace in Chicago (1895), the Swan Street entrance to the Larkin Building (1903), and the Martin House in Buffalo (1904; fig. 82), to name just five. The robust strength of the form seems especially appropriate in the vault opening in the banking room of the City

National Bank (1909) in Mason City, Iowa. Detached octagonal forms, usually lit through clerestory windows like those Richardson had used at the
Winn Memorial Library (see figs. 21–22), appear over and over again, as in
the library Wright added to his Oak Park establishment in 1898 (see fig.
73), the library at the Bagley House in Hinsdale, and in the library, sewing
room, and proposed tea house of the Glasner House in Glencoe, Illinois
(1905). The layered look characterizes much of his work of the era, as in the
Frank Thomas House in Oak Park (1901). The dominating hip roof of Richardson's railway depots occurs in works such as the Winslow House (see fig.
78), the Cheney House in Oak Park (1903), and the Cummings Real Estate
office in River Forest (1905).

Broad rectangular rooms covered with barrel vaults articulated with
transverse arches, such as those that mark some of Richardson's libraries,
appear as a playroom added to Wright's Oak Park house in 1893 and in the
opulent Dana House in Springfield (1902–5; figs. 83–84). The latter work
is particularly instructive. The layered exterior of brick, ornamental frieze,
and low gables is penetrated by a semicircular entrance arch reflected in the

82 Frank Lloyd Wright, Darwin Martin House, Buffalo, 1904, living room (from *Ausgeführte Bauten*, 1911)

reception room fireplace beyond. The arch-articulated barrel vault appears twice in the interior, in the dining room (its plan another derivation from that of the Glessner) and in the detached gallery. In each case it has been detailed so as to appear to be set as a clearly independent spatial form into a low-gabled envelope, and it is expressed externally by at least one semicircular window centered on the vault. The envelope containing the gallery is two-storied and includes at the lower level a library with bookcases set perpendicular to the long wall, forming alcoves. The relationship between barrel vault and alcove library is clearly visible in the drawing of the gallery Wright included in the German monograph of 1910 (fig. 84) and as clearly points to a Richardsonian source, such as the Ames Memorial at North Easton, Massachusetts, or the Converse Memorial Library in Malden, Massachusetts (1883–85). The photograph of the interior of the Ames Library reproduced in Richardson's monograph on his North Easton buildings, a folio probably once available to Wright because it was in Sullivan's library, may have been a source of inspiration here (see fig. 24). It shows the barrel-

83 Frank Lloyd Wright, Susan Lawrence Dana House, Springfield, Ill., 1902–5, exterior (from *Ausgeführte Bauten und Entwürfen*, 1910)

84 Frank Lloyd Wright, Dana House, gallery and library (from *Ausgeführte Bauten und Entwürfen*, 1910)

vaulted space defined by two-story alcoves as clearly independent of the gabled outer shell.

And finally, in the Arthur Heurtley House in Oak Park (1902; fig. 85), Wright seemed bent upon reworking in a domestic design and other materials the schema of the Crane Memorial Library in Quincy (see fig. 23). Not only did he appropriate the low-sprung Syrian arch for the entranceway (and living room fireplace), he reiterated Richardson's characteristic tripartite external composition (brick base, window strip, controlling roof), the repeated horizontals of water table, brickwork, coping, windows, eave, and ridge, and the contained, blocky form of the earlier building. Although the Heurtley House is unmistakably a design by Wright, it is perhaps, after the Winslow of a decade earlier, his most Richardsonian work. Perhaps it was intended, unconsciously to be sure, as a parting salute to the older man's contribution to his work, for Wright had in the preceding year or two generated a personal domestic architectural form that, while retaining thoroughly absorbed elements of Richardsonian repose, reflects the incorporation of sources other than Richardson's works and transforms the lot.

However Richardsonian the Dana or Heurtley houses, we would never mistake them for works by the older architect. Wright was a designer strong enough to transform his sources into something personal, especially after his initial decade. The strength of Wright's ego, like Sullivan's, precluded for him the role of epigone. For example, the round-arched Richardsonian entrance to the Heutley House is fronted by a small terrace defined on its forward edge by a low parapet shaped like a prow (fig. 86). This pointed projection echoes others in the plan of the house itself and is picked up in the decoration and furniture designed for it; it is also an aggressive form reminiscent of the salient common to military architecture. It both protects the entrance and suggests a defensive attitude on the part of the occupants in relation to the public sphere beyond the entry way. As in the Winslow House, we witness here the guarded privacy Wright designed into a domestic establishment; in houses after 1901 it is often difficult at first to locate the entrance. How Wright ultimately differed from Richardson as a designer is demonstrated by comparing this detail with a similar one in Richardson's work, a detail it is unlikely Wright could have known. Richardson once placed a similar defining parapet before an arch, in a prominent but nonetheless minor entry to the Paine House in Waltham, Massachusetts (see fig. 42); but in his usage, it is a fluid, curvilinear continuation of the glacial boulder wall to which it attaches, and it echoes the nearby terrace walls created by Olmsted to bind building to site (see fig. 41). Richardson's

85 Frank Lloyd Wright, Arthur Heurtley House, Oak Park, 1902, exterior (from Hitchcock, *Nature of Materials*, 1942)

86 Frank Lloyd Wright, Heurtley House, entrance detail (photo: author's collection)

parapet is—unusual for him—flaccid; Wright's, aggressive. Wright's brick parapet is rigidly geometric and suggests a programmatic attitude toward the relationship between private and public realms that Richardson's detail completely lacks. (The same contrast between nature and geometry exists unresolved in one early Wright house, that of 1895 for Chauncey Williams in River Forest, Illinois, where the angular brick base rises from a pile of glacial boulders then gives way to stucco frieze and exaggerated Richardsonian roof.) By the date of the Heurtley House, its overt Richardsonian overtones notwithstanding, Wright was clearly executing a personal architectural program.

It should be clear that Wright's appropriation of Richardsonian forms, at least soon after his initial experiments at the Falkenau houses and elsewhere, cannot be construed as copying. With Sullivan's tutelage, Wright quickly developed these characteristic features to his own ends, evoking their spirit while transforming their details as he sought his own vocabulary. By the time Wright left Sullivan, he understood not only the forms of Richardsonian discipline but their effect as well. As early as 1894, in a speech to the University Guild of Evanston, Illinois, he had employed such Richardsonian buzz words as "simplicity," "repose," and "quiet." These were achieved, he said, by "harmonizing the elements of your home, the handling of the material, the construction of the windows, doors, walls [and] roof, with the various conditions and possibilities of proportion and combination." When he returned to the same guild two years later, he brought the same message. He began in the spirit of Emerson, Whitman, and Sullivan by bashing the imitation of foreign historical forms, which he defined as "anything that one can feel quite sure happened sometime, somewhere, and was not ridiculous; anything that is not our own, anything that is not American." And once again the remedies call for work that would achieve quietude and simplicity in the face of the prevailing complexity of architectural rhetoric. By the mid-nineties Wright had adopted Richardson's emphasis on a disciplined architecture whose impact depended upon the integrated combination of elemental tectonic forms. And by the end of the decade he was ready to generate out of this and other sources an architecture all his own.

6

THE PRAIRIE HOUSE

Frank Lloyd Wright unveiled his prairie house in the February 1901 issue of Edward Bok's *Ladies' Home Journal*, a Philadelphia-based, general circulation magazine (figs. 87–88). This "city man's country house on the prairie" (in fact a repeatable cluster of four houses arranged in a "quadruple block plan") has been recognized as the first complete realization of his suburban domestic ideal. Including porch and porte cochere, the "Home in a Prairie Town" was to rise from a hearth-centered, cruciform plan with library, living room, and dining room widely opening into one another along an axis perpendicular to the street, and with porch, living room, fireplace, entry, and porte cochere stretched along offset axes parallel to the street. Above this "footprint," the house in Wright's drawings stretched broadly in repeated tripartite Richardsonian layers, all grouped around the central masonry mass. The entrance hall was to be reached through a Richardsonian archway. Within, furniture and furnishings were all designed by the architect in the spirit of the domestic Arts and Crafts movement and the contemporary trend toward simplicity. In its essential *parti*, with spaces radiating outwardly from closed core through wings to transitional areas of porch or covered carriageway to open yard (a centrifugal sweep reinforced by banks of out-swinging French doors and double casement windows), the house was a logical step beyond the McAfee and Husser houses of the previous decade (see figs. 80–81). While it was heir to a domestic planning process as old as American architecture, and though it was rooted in a profound understanding of Richardson's work, it was also a completely Wrightian design.

The project unveiled in the *Ladies' Home Journal* was the first of a series of built and unbuilt prairie houses Wright designed in the next decade and a half that mark the culmination of his earlier efforts. Many are variations of the *Ladies' Home Journal* model: the Bradley House at Kankakee, Illinois (1900), the Henderson House in Elmhurst (1901), and even, greatly expanded, the justly famous Darwin Martin House in Buffalo (see fig. 82).

In the Ward Willits House in Highland Park, Illinois (1901), Wright first built the fully articulated cruciform plan (figs. 89–90), with entry in one wing, living room in a second, dining room occupying a third, and utility spaces in a fourth, all grouped around a central masonry stack of fireplaces. Subsequent houses, ranging from square to cruciform plans, almost all have

87 Frank Lloyd Wright, "Home in a Prairie Town," perspective (from *Ladies' Home Journal,* 1901)

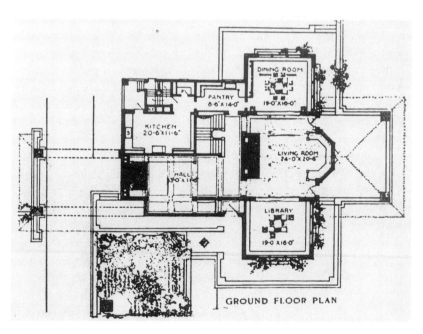

88 Frank Lloyd Wright, "Home in a Prairie Town," plan (from *Ladies' Home Journal,* 1901)

a masonry core, and most develop three-dimensionally into spreading masses through the use of pronounced horizontal lines. Some major examples, other than the Martin and Willits houses, include the Gilmore House in Madison, Wisconsin (1908), and in Illinois, the Cheney House, Oak Park, and Francis Little House, Peoria (both 1904), the Robie House,

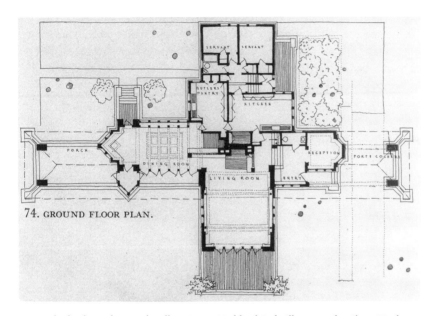

74. GROUND FLOOR PLAN.

89 Frank Lloyd Wright, Ward Willits House, Highland Park, Ill., 1901, plan (from Hitchcock, *Nature of Materials*, 1942)

90 Frank Lloyd Wright, Willits House, exterior (from Hitchcock, *Nature of Materials*, 1942)

Chicago (1906; see fig. 93), the Coonley House in Riverside (1907; see fig. 97), and the Roberts House, River Forest (1908; fig. 91).

Just as Richardson had his "lengthened shadow," his followers who turned his beloved Romanesque forms into a source for repeated Richardsonian designs from Massachusetts to Texas and beyond, so Wright, too, was surrounded by a group of designers now known as the Prairie school. These architects, many of whom Wright had employed in his Oak Park studio, spread the prairie house from the shores at Wood's Hole, Massachusetts, to the hills of Oregon in a series of works, some rivaling those of the man who had himself now become master, some merely aping them. The best of these were Walter Burley Griffin, William Purcell, George Elmslie, and George Maher. As Wright was never generous in recognizing his antecedents, so he never gracefully accepted his followers. His second *Architectural Record* article, "In the Cause of Architecture" (1914), lashed out against the lot of them. They were nonetheless, like Wright himself, creative heirs to Richardson's legacy and more.

91 Frank Lloyd Wright, Isabel Roberts House, River Forest, Ill., 1908, living room (from Hitchcock, *Nature of Materials*, 1942)

As Norris Kelly Smith has emphasized, Wright, when he introduced his mature work to the professional readership in his first *Architectural Record* article, "In the Cause of Architecture" (1908), described it as both radical and dedicated to the "cause conservative." The conservative element in Wright's mature early work had an almost endless variety of strands, from the domestic to the exotic, from the recent to the distant. During the course of his extraordinarily long career, Wright was to draw upon a bewildering variety of sources for his ideas, sources European, Oriental, and native American from both above and below the border. Most of these exotic elements became important after the period of his career that captures our attention here, but one interest was to parallel his tutelage under Richardson and Sullivan. Wright was already aware in the mid-1890s of the nonwestern sources that were to become increasingly important in his work. The Ho-o-den at the World's Columbian Exposition in Chicago in 1893 has frequently been mentioned as his introduction to Japanese architecture. Traces of its influence can be found in works from about 1900, as in the Foster House in Chicago, and, perhaps, the Bradley and Hickox houses in Kankakee, Illinois. In 1905 he visited Japan, and thereafter an Oriental sense invades some of the presentation drawings prepared for Wright by his assistant, Marion Mahony. Wright always insisted that it was the lesson of elimination in the Japanese woodblock print, of which he was to become a busy collector and dealer, that caught his attention, not Japanese architecture. This lesson is perhaps most apparent in the broad stucco planes and flat detailing of his houses after 1900 (although these may owe as much to the influence of the Viennese Joseph M. Olbrich, whose work Wright drew upon for aspects of his design of the Larkin Building in Buffalo and elsewhere, and certainly find their parallels in some aspects of contemporary Craftsman work). In 1916, beyond the period of our concern, Wright left for an extended stay in Japan.

Wright's intense investigation of Richardson's achievement and his courting of more exotic muses did not blind him to other traditional American sources of inspiration. The hearth-centered, centrifugal domestic plan that he used embryonically in his own house of 1889, in the Winslow House in 1893 (see fig. 77), and characteristically in his residential designs of the next decade (see fig. 89), owes little to Richardson, although some of its elements, such as the open plan and the focal fireplace, were available in the shingle-style houses of Richardson, Silsbee, and others. Rather, it springs from deep in the nineteenth century. While we think of the characteristic eighteenth-century Georgian or Federal house plan as centered

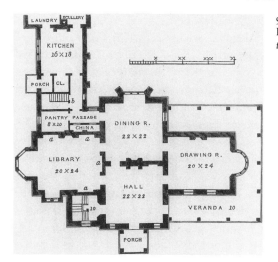

92 A. J. Downing, Lake or River Villa, plan (*The Architecture of Country Houses*, 1850)

upon a void, the ceremonial stair hall that axially divides one side of a square or rectangular house from the other, an alternate domestic planning tradition placed the masonry stack at the center of the composition. Among Thomas Jefferson's surviving sketches for Monticello and other domestic designs, for example, are cruciform and hearth-centered residential plans. This type surfaces over and over again in the suburban and rural house pattern books of the nineteenth century. Quick grazing through this literature finds the cruciform in one or more examples in A. J. Davis's *Rural Residences* (1837), W. H. Ranlett's *Architect* (1847–49), A. J. Downing's *Architecture of Country Houses* (1850; fig. 92), Gervaise Wheeler's *Homes for the People* (1855), G. E. Woodward's *Cottages and Farmhouses* (1867), and I. H. Hobbs's *Architecture* (1873). A central masonry stack or group of stacks is common to most of these cruciform examples, and the description in the Hobbs publication of the plan of the suburban Jackson House erected near Pittsburgh, for example, includes this prescription for a proto-Wrightian, centrifugal, open interior: "the hall, dining-room, sitting-room, and parlor, can be thrown into one grand room . . . connected with back and front porches by windows running to the floor." A host of parallel designs could be cited. We should not picture Wright at any time rifling through these books in search of an appropriate geometric shape, and in any event the three-dimensional realization of any of them would have caused him to shudder. The type reached him as a common and traditional one; to know it he had no need to ransack the architectural libraries of his day.

In any event, the focal fire as symbol of home is ages old, and this symbol was reinvigorated during the nineteenth century. The sources for the spreading, hearth-centered, suburban or rural domestic ideal extend beyond architectural publications into the realm of nineteenth-century literature. Henry Wadsworth Longfellow, Charles Dudley Warner, and many others found it a symbolic focus for literary works. In his *Autobiography* Wright listed Herman Melville, for example, as among a motley (and grossly incomplete) assortment of writers whose work he "long ago consulted and occasionally remembered." Only one story by Melville could have remotely influenced Wright, "I and My Chimney" published in *Putnam's Monthly Magazine* for March 1856. How Wright might have come across this piece, if indeed he did, is anyone's guess (since scarcely anyone read Melville until his "rediscovery" in the 1920s), but the proto-Thurberesque battle of the sexes that constitutes the action of Melville's paper is cast in architecturally symbolic terms that are also proto-Wrightian.

The narrator lives in an old farmhouse (based on Melville's Arrowhead at Pittsfield, Massachusetts) whose rooms on each level group themselves around a vast masonry mass riddled with fireplaces. His wife and daughters want to improve the place by ripping out this monster and creating an open hall. Melville goes beyond this Freudian conflict, however, to describe the house as not merely rural but anti-urban. In the cities the houses are tall and thin; they are confining. This house is, in contrast, wide, having been built where there is plenty of room, and it is set amid scenic richness. The chimney, "a free citizen of this free land," is the center of domestic life, and in fact it assumes for Melville here an almost sacral significance as a "grand high altar." The oversized fireplace stack in the prairie house was not only the age-old symbol of domesticity. It assumed for Wright something of the same character—Norris Kelly Smith has called it "sacramental"—that Melville gave to his narrator's chimney. With neither Melville nor Wright is there anything new here, of course, as they both reflect the nineteenth-century cult of domesticity, which reemphasized the hearth-centered suburban focus of family life in contrast to the commercial world of the downtown office blocks.

Whatever the deep and broad historical and cultural sources that enter into the makeup of the prairie house (Melville's story being but one example of the kind of literary source available), Wright did not forsake the lessons of his Richardsonian apprenticeship. Any study of the plans Wright designed in these early years of the twentieth century demonstrates that they are for the most part variations on two themes. The one is an implacably symmetrical *parti*, such as we find it in the River Forest Golf Club (1901) and other public works. The other is used for most of the residential designs and consists of an axial alignment, usually of library, living room, and dining room, as in the *Ladies' Home Journal* project (see fig. 88), plus, commonly, utility areas more loosely arranged. A variation of the latter type aligns spaces along offset axes, as in the relationship of porch and dining room in the Ward Willits House in Highland Park (see fig. 89), which generates in two dimensions an interplay of symmetry and asymmetry that is picked up in three dimensions by the interplay of one- and two-story wings. In almost any of these mature prairie houses a balanced element has been set within an unbalanced whole. Thus the forward projecting, living room wing of the Willits House is almost classical in its balanced composition, but it fronts an unbalanced perpendicular wing that pierces it horizontally (see fig. 90). Here we see Wright building creatively upon the symmetrical-asymmetrical interplay characteristic of Richardson's work.

As with Sullivan's Wainwright Building, which not surprisingly shows traces of the architect's concurrent study of Richardson's work, so the prairie house shows Wright's prolonged investigation of Richardsonian design. And like the Wainwright, the prairie house is profoundly different from anything Richardson achieved because it was designed in an era in which new materials and constructional technology permitted a fresh attitude toward structure, resulting in an opening of form never contemplated by the older architect. Wright's emphatic horizontals—the long spans, pronounced cantilevers, cruciform plans, open interiors, and dynamic three dimensional forms of the characteristic prairie house—owe nothing to the closed, conventionally load-bearing blocks typical of Richardson (see fig. 34). Wright's daring exploitation of the cantilever, as in the extraordinary overhangs of the Mrs. Thomas Gale House in Oak Park, Illinois (1904–9), or the Robie House (fig. 93), was made possible largely because of the availability of steel, the structural use of which, as we have seen, postdated the work of his predecessor. Where Richardson had occasionally produced a broadly continuous interior room (fig. 43), as in the Paine House livinghall (by supporting the main beam from the roof structure by means of an iron tension rod), Wright now habitually created coherently expansive interiors extending through the outer walls by means of casements, floor-to-soffit doors, porches, and overhangs to embrace the great outdoors.

While it is essential to mark the similarities between Richardson and Wright, it is equally essential to recognize the historically profound differences that exist between the two. While both architects must be discussed against the backdrop of the English and American Arts and Crafts movement, for example, Richardson, as we can judge from his library and his work (especially his decorative designs ranging from furniture to appointments, as in the New York State Court of Appeals in Albany, 1876–81), was at home in the preindustrial ideology of John Ruskin and William Morris (whose books he owned). Wright, while his connection to C. R. Ashbee and other Arts-and-Craftsmen is firmly documented, eschewed neither the machine nor its structural products. His talk at Hull-House in 1901 on "The

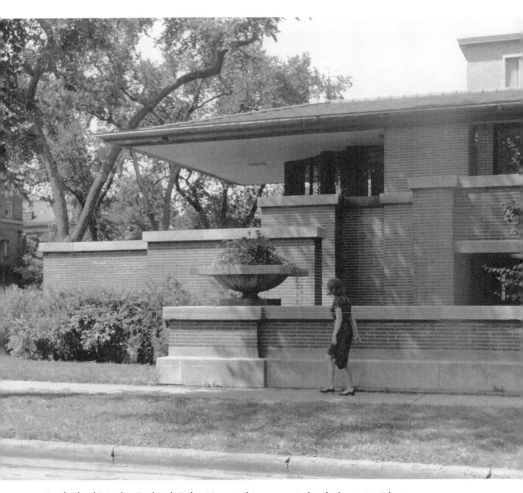

93 Frank Lloyd Wright, Frederick Robie House, Chicago, 1906, detail of exterior (photo: Jean Baer O'Gorman)

Art and Craft of the Machine" may be cited as key testimony to Wright's Janus-headed position at the turn of the century. On one side, he looked deeply if selectively into the nineteenth century, in part through Sullivan's and Richardson's eyes; and on the other, he regarded quite receptively the mechanical and structural transformations provided by burgeoning American industry. In architectural terms, the result was the opening up (or as he was later to say, "destruction") of the Richardsonian box in the prairie house.

In his *Architectural Record* article of 1908, his definitive statement of intention from this period, Wright rooted architecture in nature and pronounced "a sense of the organic" as "indispensable to an architect." In this he was again an heir to the nineteenth century in general and Sullivan in particular, and through Sullivan, to the tradition of conventionalized ornamental design exemplified by nineteenth-century theorists. (According to his own later testimony, Wright in these years was familiar with Owen Jones's *Grammar of Ornament*.) In the first important notice of Wright's career, a 1900 article by his colleague Robert Spencer in the *Architectural Review*, this source of Wright's ornament is made evident. "It is certainly true that the highly conventionalized, the quiet, consistent structural element, is always present in his compositions, modifying and quieting the most naturalistic motives," Spencer wrote. "Nature, who knows the most rigid and subtle geometry, as well as the most voluptuous freedom of . . . form, is the source to which he has always gone for inspiration." And, Spencer notes, it was Sullivan who drew Wright's attention to this design process. Where Furness had once filled his sketchbooks with graphite studies of the lilies of his garden, searching for this organizational geometry, and Sullivan had probed a specimen lotus for its structural principles, Wright employed photographic studies of wildflowers to the same ends. As we have seen, Ruskin called this process "gathering" and "governing," and examples by Wright of each of these stages are found in William C. Gannett's *House Beautiful* (1896–97), a work published by the architect and his client William Winslow. The book contains photographs taken by Wright that show him "gathering" among the wildflowers (fig. 94), and it contains decorative borders and other devices that are line drawings by Wright composed in part of "governed" or geometrically altered natural forms (fig. 95). Here are the lineal descendants of conventionalized floral designs by Furness (see fig. 47) and Sullivan (see figs. 49 and 51). By means of this process, the designer put his natural source through what Wright called, in a lecture at the Art Institute of Chicago in 1900, "a rare and difficult process" in which the "life principle of the flower is translated to terms of building stone," and this is "conventionalization, and it is poetry."

In his prairie houses and other works of the first decade and a half of the twentieth century, Wright sought to extend this geometrical-poetical principle from the individual flower as source for ornamental embellishment to the total environment as inspiration for the complete architectural organism. The prairie house was filled almost from the beginning with accents—"art glass" windows, ornamental friezes, decorative panels—that contain forms derived from the conventionalization of botanical specimens. Mature examples of these are usually angular analogies, exemplifying

94 Frank Lloyd Wright, photo of wild flowers (William C. Gannett, *The House Beautiful,* 1896–97)

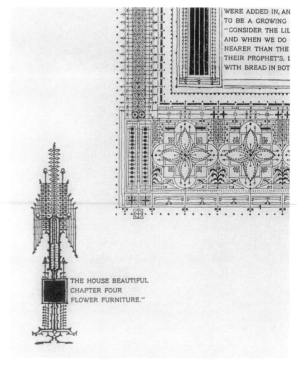

95 Frank Lloyd Wright, ornamental detail (William C. Gannett, *The House Beautiful,* 1896–97)

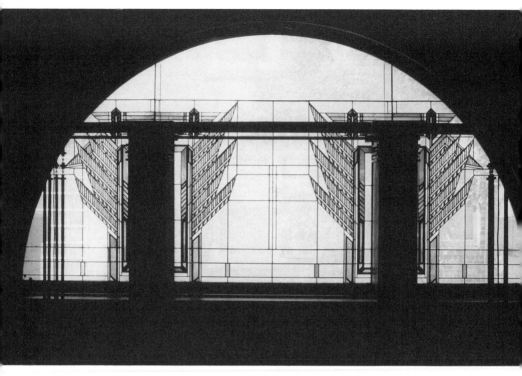

96 Frank Lloyd Wright, Dana House, sumac glass in dining room (photo: Donald Hoffmann)

Wright's tendency "to draw away from . . . [Sullivan's] efflorescence toward the straight line and rectangular pattern" generated by the use of T-square and triangle, as he was to write in *Genius and the Mobocracy*. In its original condition, the Dana House in Springfield, Illinois (see fig. 83), was, as were most of the prairie houses, richly provided inside and out with planters and urns filled with vegetation having its artistic analogy on the exterior frieze and in leaded glass embellished with conventionalized patterns of sumac (fig. 96), as well as in windows and lamps bedecked with geometric butter-flies. The colorful exterior frieze of plaster and tile of the Avery Coonley House of 1907 in Riverside, Illinois, sports a repetitive pattern of conventionalized tulips (fig. 97). Each "tulip" is composed of a vertical "stem" forming a central axis to each side of which rectangular "flowers" and "leafs" are balanced. However much it seems to anticipate the neoplasticism of twentieth-century Dutch artists like Piet Mondrian or Theo van Doesburg, it is a direct if evolved, straight-lined, and rectangular descendent of the curvilinear floral patterns of the window tympani flanking the central *pavillon* of Furness's Pennsylvania Academy in Philadelphia (see fig. 48).

In Wright's mind, the prairie house seemed a visual fugue in which these ornamental incidents were minor echoes of the major theme of the house. For Wright, conventionalization was an idea applicable not just to ornamental details. It embodied the complete architectural environment. In a speech to the Architectural League at the Chicago Art Institute as early as 1900, he adapted the specific process of conventionalization to the totality of architectural design. "Architecture is the most complete of conventionalizations," he wrote in the *Architectural Record* article of 1908. What he meant by this is perhaps best exemplified among his early works by the windmill he erected for his aunts at Spring Green, Wisconsin, in 1897 (figs. 98–99). In Wright's mind, architecture and technology were congruent in this design and conventionalized from nature, although in this case the primary analogy is with animal rather than vegetable forms. Wright, who was frequently to provide romantic names for his designs, called his tower Romeo and Juliet, because, as he explained in his *Autobiography*, he thought of its

97 Frank Lloyd Wright, Avery Coonley House, Riverside, Ill., 1907, detail of exterior (from Hitchcock, *Nature of Materials*, 1942)

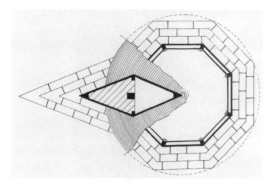

98 Frank Lloyd Wright, Romeo and Juliet, Spring Green, Wis., 1897, plan (from Wright, *A Testament*, 1957)

interlocking shapes as an entwined, mutually supportive couple. Romeo is the lozenge-shaped spine that surrounds and stiffens an internal shaft that carries the rotating blades; Juliet is the octagonal stairtower that receives the thrust of and in turn strengthens the spine. To this primary anthropomorphic analogy Wright added a secondary botanical one, for he likened the floors to horizontal membranes that strengthen a hollow plant stem from within. Whether or not the structure as built works this way is immaterial; it was Wright's designing intention that it should. He was later, in skyscraper projects of the 1920s and in the Johnson Wax Tower in Racine, Wisconsin (1944), the Price Tower in Bartlesville, Oklahoma (1952), and "The Illinois," the projected mile-high publicity stunt of his last years, to exploit fully the analogy of the tree with its continuous structure of taproot, central trunk, and cantilevered limbs, abandoning completely the "inorganic" metal frame composed of additive, riveted pieces. These were the ultimate developments of the conventionalization of nature that had reached Wright from the nineteenth century through Sullivan.

The emphatic horizontal look of the houses of Wright's early maturity (or of the Prairie school in general) displays a debt to Richardson, and more. Both architects equated the level line with quietude. But the degree to which Wright emphasized this direction both within and without his houses stems also from the generalized environment for which his houses were intended. "We of the Middle West are living on the prairie. The prairie has a beauty of its own and we should . . . accentuate this natural beauty, its quiet level," he wrote in the first installment of "In the Cause of Architecture." The strength of Wright's purpose transforms the Richardsonian device and makes it his own. Not all Wright houses were built on the wide open spaces of the Midwest. The Robie House in southside Chicago (see fig.

99 Frank Lloyd Wright, Romeo and Juliet, exterior (from Hitchcock, *Nature of Materials*, 1942)

93), most famous house of this period, is on a corner urban lot (as is the Meyer May House in Grand Rapids, Michigan, 1908). The unexecuted Metzger House of 1902 for Sault Ste Marie, Michigan, was an expanded version of the *Ladies' Home Journal* design intended to be perched on an elevated site (as was the executed Gilmore House in Madison, Wisconsin). And the midland prairie cannot be extended eastward to western New York state, where Wright built some important houses early in the century (see fig. 82), or westward to Montecito, California, where he erected the Stewart House in 1909. But in Wright's usage the prairie was as much concept as actual topography, as much a locus of the mind as a characteristic of the land. He sought to celebrate poetically the broad expansiveness of the vast Midwest, much as Sullivan had sought to emphasize poetically the essence of tallness in buildings such as the Guaranty in Buffalo (see fig. 63). In his vertically articulated urban block Sullivan had transformed the Philadelphia midcentury commercial facade; in his horizontally extended houses Wright transformed the Richardsonian layered look.

It was characteristic of Wright, then, to see the whole of the inland plain conventionalized in the spreading horizontals of the prairie house exterior or the continuous expanses of its girded interiors, and to see his ornamental details as conventionalized native plantlife. He was heir to an ideal unity of architecture and nature that sprang in this country from Jeffersonian ideals and marked the works of the erstwhile teams of Downing and Davis, and Olmsted and Richardson. In a sense he merged Richardson's geological analogy in works like the Ames Gate Lodge (see fig. 38) with the tradition of conventionalization learned at Sullivan's drafting board and with the potentials of the new technology to achieve what he called an "organic" architecture—an architecture, as he said, "of" the land, not "on" it. The result was the celebration of place (even if that place was a poetic concept rather than a physical location) that is the prairie house, a domestic architectural form that evolved out of the past to become truly his own. It was here that he put his personal stamp upon an entire building type.

The myriad conservative strands that Wright wove into his own personal architecture are perhaps best illustrated and summed up in the crowning achievement in domestic design from the early period in his career. This work was his own in every sense of the word, for it was the country retreat he erected for himself on family lands just south of the Wisconsin River near Spring Green in 1911 (rebuilt 1914 to 1915 after the original had been destroyed by arson and rebuilt again after another fire on a more expansive scale from 1925 onward). Taliesin (figs. 100–101; also figs. 104–105), as

100 Frank Lloyd Wright, Taliesin, Spring Green, Wis., 1911 on, exterior (photo: author)

101 Frank Lloyd Wright, Taliesin, Spring Green, living room (photo: Ezra Stoller © ESTO)

Wright called his house-studio-farm of wood, plaster, and stone, hangs on the brow of a ledge above the valley, its multiple hips echoing the surrounding hills, its golds, browns, yellows, and reds echoing the seasonal colors of the landscape, its interiors enriched by Wright's collection of Oriental objets d'art. In a sense this was the most conservative work of his career, for it recapitulated the development of American rural domestic design from Jefferson's Monticello onward, including the environmental concerns of Downing and Davis and Olmsted, the formal discipline and geological analogy of Richardson, and the conventionalization of nature in the works of Sullivan and his sources. At the same time, it was a house only Wright's "peculiar genius," as the *Architectural Record* labeled it in 1911, could have conceived.

Wright had already provided the ancestral lands near Spring Green with his Hillside Home School of 1901, a conventionalized outcropping of rock-faced limestone ashlar in which Richardson's Ames Monument merged with his Woodland Station and was transformed by Wright's maturing sense of geometry, space, and proportion. Now he returned to a hillside nearer the Wisconsin River to add his own habitation. At Taliesin, Wright was to carry on the ideal of integrated private life, professionalism, and play that had marked his own earlier Oak Park arrangement and Richardson's establishment before him. In Brookline and at Taliesin, the workrooms were strung out like a tail attached to the domestic quarters. But Wright's was the more integrated and the more mature ensemble. Certainly here was a domestic type Melville would have understood; certainly this was the house prescribed by Emerson, whom Wright was quoting at least as early as 1900 (although he typically fails to mention the writer among his consultants in the *Autobiography*). In "Self-Reliance" the essayist assured his readers that "if the American artist will study with hope and love the precise thing to be done by him, considering the climate, the soil, the length of day, the wants of the people, the habit and form of government, he will create a house in which these will find themselves fitted, and taste and sentiment will be satisfied too." Taliesin to a greater extent than any other of Wright's works to 1915 embodied conceptions of family, society, politics, environment, history, and conventionalized nature, as well as "taste and sentiment."

Taliesin expressed that ideal of agrarian democracy, a combination of culture and agriculture, that Wright probably derived from Jefferson, a source of ideas he recognizes with the same ambiguity he applied to Richardson. If Wright did not learn of the statesman's works from his writings (although

102 Thomas Jefferson, Monticello, near Charlottesville, Va., 1767 on, view (photo: author)

103 Thomas Jefferson, Monticello, entrance hall (photo: James T. Tkatch, courtesy the Thomas Jefferson Memorial Foundation, Inc.)

there are passages in his own publications from these years that suggest Wright knew something of Jefferson's social politics), then he did from Jefferson's own home at Monticello (figs. 102–103). The two-story living room with half-octagonal balcony of the cruciform Isabel Roberts House (see fig. 91) suggests that Wright knew the identical spatial conformation (with very different details) in the hall at cruciform Monticello. Like Jefferson's perpetual "putting up, and pulling down" at Monticello, Wright was continuously altering and expanding Taliesin out of necessity or desire. Like Monticello, Taliesin is not merely rural, it is anti-urban. Like Monticello, the house at Taliesin was conceptually one-storied, with its wings wrapped around its hillside site just below the summit (compare figs. 100 and 102). Like Monticello, the interior of Taliesin joined its surroundings through tall openings leading onto terraces overlooking the rolling terrain. Like Monticello, Taliesin is not a mere building but an entire environment in which man, architecture, and nature form a harmonious whole. There is at Taliesin Wright's own summing-up of the role of man in nature that stems ultimately from the age of romanticism.

Jefferson was, of course, bound at Monticello by the universal chains of dogmatic Palladian classicism, although he struggled mightily against them, and to a certain degree he achieved within the system an elasticity corresponding to his vision of place. Wright was heir to the picturesque tradition of Downing and Davis, in which classical forms gave way to irregular, asymmetrical, and natural elements. This can be seen, for example, in the correspondences of architecture and place found in the hearth-centered, cruciform plan with asymmetrical utility wing and unbalanced medieval pile of the "Lake or River Villa for a Picturesque Site" in Downing's *Architecture of Country Houses* (see fig. 92), or in Davis's neo-Gothic Lyndhurst at Tarrytown, New York (1838–65). Taliesin connects with Monticello through intervening works such as Richardson's Bigelow and Paine houses, and Davis's Lyndhurst.

If Jefferson had been tied to the classical tradition, Downing and Davis in their turn were equally committed to the picturesque Gothic and other revived medieval styles in their books and buildings. As we have seen, Richardson drew upon the achievements of Downing and Davis while working within the natural environmental framework espoused by Olmsted, and in his mature suburban and rural designs he drew not only upon architectural history but natural history as well. In works such as the Ames Gate Lodge (fig. 38), Paine House (fig. 41), or Gurney House, which were definitive, we remember, only because of his premature death, he created tentative geological analogies that were relaxed variants on the conventionalizations from nature of mid-nineteenth-century ornamental theorists. Wright followed suit. The broad exterior of Taliesin was composed of horizontal layers of continuous windows above unbroken stucco or stone and beneath long, low hips extending far beyond the walls (fig. 104). As we have seen, Wright was thus opening up the tripartite compositional format developed by Richardson in works such as the suburban libraries.

The low wings of Taliesin sweeping around the brow of its hillside site were interrupted periodically by broad chimneys harboring domestic fires within the living spaces and pinning the horizontal hip roofs to the sloping site without. These were sturdy, vertical stacks of masonry in which local

104 Frank Lloyd Wright, Taliesin, Spring Green, exterior (*Architectural Record*, 1913; photo courtesy Domino's Center for Architecture and Design)

limestone was laid in level, rock-faced courses with an occasional stone pulled forward two to three inches to create a pattern of shadow (fig. 105). Here Richardsonian sources join Wright's training under Sullivan, for this was a conventionalized geological analogy: with each stone laid by the mason in its original bedded position, the walls recreate sections cut through a quarry. The pattern was a geometrical governing of the natural strata from which the stone was gathered.

Taliesin was the crowning achievement of Wright's early work. It brought together the many strands of the past; it embodied a deep sense of history; it was the culmination of a search for a personal and a landed domestic architecture that began before Wright was born.

105 Frank Lloyd Wright, Taliesin, Spring Green, detail of exterior stonework (*Architectural Record*, 1913; photo courtesy Domino's Center for Architecture and Design)

GLOSSARY

Aedicule. The frame of an opening with two columns, piers, or pilasters supporting a gable, lintel, or entablature and pediment.

Archivolt. The continuous molding following the contour (or *Intrados*) of an arch.

Arcuated. Arched construction, as opposed to *trabeated*, or post and lintel, construction.

Ashlar. Cut masonry in which the stones, while they may be rough faced, have even sides and square edges. *Random ashlar* exhibits discontinuous vertical and horizontal joints; *horizontal ashlar* exhibits discontinuous vertical and continuous horizontal joints.

Astylar. A facade without the articulation of columns, piers, or pilasters.

Bay. The basic spatial unit of plan, elevation, or structural system marked by fenestration, supports, vaulting, etc.

Belt course. A horizontal molding or run of decoration stretching across a facade.

Belvedere. A small lookout tower above a roof.

Box girder. In iron or steel frame construction, a hollow horizontal member composed of two vertical and two horizontal plates forming in cross section an open quadrangle.

Cantilever. A horizontal structural member visually supported only at one end.

Casement. A side-hinged window that swings open like a door.

Chancel. That part of a church in which the choir and main altar are located.

Coping. The topmost course in a wall, designed to shed water.

Cornice. The projecting decorative molding along the top of a wall or building.

En loge. A French term meaning, literally, "in a box." Students at the Ecole des Beaux-Arts sketched preliminary competitive designs in isolated alcoves.

Esquisse. French for "sketch," or preliminary design.

Extrados. The curving outer line of an arch. See *Intrados.*

Frieze. A horizontal band of decoration along the top of a wall.

Half-timber. Frame construction in which the wooden members are exposed externally and infilled with stucco or masonry, or a decorative pattern suggesting such construction.

Hip roof. A roof of four, usually gentle, slopes.

Inglenook. A recess containing a bench or benches before a fireplace.

Intrados. The inner curve or underside of an arch. See *Extrados.*

Jamb. The side of a window, doorway, or other opening.

Lintel. A horizontal member bridging an opening.

Lucarne. A dormer the face of which is often an extension of the plane of the facade below.

Mansard. A high, visible roof composed of planes of two different slopes.

Mullion. A vertical member dividing a window into panes. See *Transom.*

Nave. The principal congregational space in a church.

Oriel. A bay window; an angular or curved projection filled with fenestration.

Palladian window. A classical composition divided into three parts: a wide arched opening in the center flanked by lower, narrower trabeated openings.

Parapet. A low wall marking the edge of a roof, terrace, etc.

Pargetting. Exterior ornamental stuccowork.

Parti. A French term for the basic scheme of an architectural design.

Pavillon. French for "pavilion," a projecting subdivision of a building, usually square in plan and often capped by a mansard roof, commonly found at the center or sides of an elevation.

Piazza. In the United States, a veranda or porch.

Pier. A vertical support that is square in plan.

Porte cochere. A porch covering a vehicular entrance.

Salient. A central, projecting subdivision of a wall.

Salle des pas perdus. French, literally "hall of lost steps." The large circulatory space found in the center of some plans arranged according to the principles of the Ecole des Beaux-Arts.

Soffit. The underside of an architectural element such as an eave or an arch.

Spandrel. In frame construction, the horizontal member visible on the facade.

Trabeated. Post and lintel construction, as opposed to *arcuated.*

Transept. The transverse arm of a cross-shaped church.

Transom. The horizontal member dividing a window into panes. See *Mullion.*

Transverse arch. An arch dividing a vault into bays.

Tympanum. The area between the lintel of a doorway and the arch above it.

Voussoir. The wedge-shaped stone used in the construction of an arch.

Water table. The flared base of a wall.

SELECTED READING

RICHARDSON

Hitchcock, Henry-Russell. *The Architecture of H. H. Richardson and His Times.* New York, 1936 (and later editions).

————. *Richardson as a Victorian Architect*, Northampton, Mass., 1966.

Larson, Paul Clifford, and Susan M. Brown, eds. *The Spirit of H. H. Richardson on the Midland Prairies.* Ames, Iowa, 1988.

Ochsner, Jeffrey Karl. *H. H. Richardson: Complete Architectural Works.* Cambridge, Mass., 1982; augmented ed., 1984.

O'Gorman, James F. "Henry Hobson Richardson and Frank Lloyd Wright." *Art Quarterly* 32 (Autumn 1969): 292–315.

————. *H. H. Richardson: Architectural Forms for an American Society.* Chicago, 1987.

————. *Henry Hobson Richardson and His Office: Selected Drawings.* Cambridge, Mass., 1974.

Quinan, Jack. "H. H. Richardson and the Boston Granite Tradition." *Little Journal of the S.A.H. Western New York Chapter* 3 (February 1979): 20–29.

Scully, Vincent J., Jr. *The Shingle Style: Architectural Theory and Design from Richardson to the Origins of Wright.* New Haven, Conn., 1955; rev. ed., 1974.

Van Rensselaer, Mariana Griswold. *Henry Hobson Richardson and His Works.* Boston, 1888 (and modern reprints).

SULLIVAN

Andrew, David S. *Louis Sullivan and the Polemics of Modern Architecture.* Urbana and Chicago, 1985.

Manson, Grant. "Sullivan and Wright: An Uneasy Union of Celts," *Architectural Review* 118 (November 1955): 297–300.

Menocal, Narciso G. *Architecture as Nature: The Transcendentalist Idea of Louis Sullivan.* Madison, Wis., 1981.

Morrison, Hugh. *Louis Sullivan: Prophet of Modern Architecture.* New York, 1935 (and later reprint).

Paul, Sherman. *Louis Sullivan: An Architect in American Thought.* Englewood Cliffs, N.J., 1962.

Sprague, Paul. *The Drawings of Louis Henry Sullivan.* Princeton, N.J., 1979.

Sullivan, Louis H. *The Autobiography of an Idea.* New York, 1924 (and later reprints).

———. *Kindergarten Chats and Other Writings.* New York, 1947.

———. *A System of Architectural Ornament According with a Philosophy of Man's Powers.* New York, 1924 (and later reprints).

Szarkowski, John. *The Idea of Louis Sullivan.* Minneapolis, 1956.

Twombly, Robert. *Louis Sullivan: His Life and Work.* New York, 1986.

Twombly, Robert, ed. *Louis Sullivan: The Public Papers.* Chicago, 1988.

Weisman, Winston. "Philadelphia Functionalism and Sullivan." *Journal of the Society of Architectural Historians* 20 (March 1961): 3–19.

De Wit, Wim, ed. *Louis Sullivan: The Function of Ornament.* Chicago, 1986. (See especially David Van Zanten, "Sullivan to 1890," and William H. Jordy, "The Tall Buildings.")

Wright, Frank Lloyd. *Genius and the Mobocracy.* New York, 1949 (and later reprints).

WRIGHT

Ashbee, C. R. "Taliesin." *Western Architect* 19 (February 1913): 16–19.

Bolon, Carol R., Robert S. Nelson, and Linda Seidel, eds. *The Nature of Frank Lloyd Wright.* Chicago, 1988. (See especially Joseph Connors, "Wright on Nature and the Machine.").

Brooks. H. Allen. *The Prairie School: Frank Lloyd Wright and His Midwest Contemporaries.* Toronto, 1976.

Eaton, Leonard. *Two Chicago Architects and Their Clients: Frank Lloyd Wright and Howard Van Doren Shaw.* Cambridge, Mass., 1969.

Fitch, James M. "Architects of Democracy: Jefferson and Wright." In his *Architecture and the Esthetics of Plenty,* 31–45. New York, 1961.

Gutheim, Frederick, ed. *Frank Lloyd Wright: Selected Writings, 1894–1940.* New York, 1941.

Hanks, David. *The Decorative Designs of Frank Lloyd Wright.* New York, 1979.

Hitchcock, Henry-Russell. *In the Nature of Materials: The Buildings of Frank Lloyd Wright, 1887–1941.* New York, 1942.

Hoffmann, Donald. *Frank Lloyd Wright: Architecture and Nature.* New York, 1986.

Manson, Grant. *Frank Lloyd Wright to 1910.* New York, 1958.

Quinan, Jack. *Frank Lloyd Wrights' Larkin Building.* Cambridge, Mass., 1987.

———. "Frank Lloyd Wright in 1893: The Chicago Context." In Bruce Brooks Pfeiffer and Gerald Nordland, eds., *Frank Lloyd Wright: In the Realm of Ideas,* 119–32. Carbondale and Edwardsville, Ill., 1988.

Scully, Vincent. "American Houses: Thomas Jefferson to Frank Lloyd Wright." In Edgar Kaufmann, Jr., ed., *The Rise of American Architecture,* 163–209. New York, 1970.

Smith, Norris Kelly. *Frank Lloyd Wright: A Study in Architectural Content.* Englewood Cliffs, N.J., 1966.

Spencer, Robert C., Jr. "The Work of Frank Lloyd Wright." *Architectural Review* 7 (June 1900): 61–72 (reissued Park Forest, Ill., 1964).

Storrer, William Allin. *The Architecture of Frank Lloyd Wright: A Complete Catalogue.* 2d ed. Cambridge, Mass., 1978.

"The Studio Home of Frank Lloyd Wright." *Architectural Record* 33 (January 1913): 45–54.

Twombly, Robert C. *Frank Lloyd Wright: His Life and His Architecture.* New York, 1979.

White, Morton, and Lucia White. *The Intellectual Versus the City, from Thomas Jefferson to Frank Lloyd Wright.* New York, 1962.

Wright, Frank Lloyd. *An Autobiography.* New York, 1943 (orig. ed., 1932; and later reprints).

———. *Ausgeführte Bauten und Entwürfen.* Berlin, 1910 (and later reprints).

———. *Ausgeführte Bauten.* Berlin, 1911 (and later reprints).

OTHER

Fein, Albert. *Frederick Law Olmsted and the American Environmental Tradition.* New York, 1972.

Jordy, William. *American Buildings and Their Architects: Progressive and Academic Ideals at the Turn of the Twentieth Century* (esp. chaps. 1–3). Garden City, N.Y., 1976.

Mumford, Lewis. *The Brown Decades.* New York, 1931 (and later editions).

O'Gorman, James F. *The Architecture of Frank Furness.* Philadelphia, 1973 (another edition, 1987).

Weingarden, Lauren S. "Naturalized Naturalism: A Ruskinian Discourse on the Search for an American Style of Architecture." *Winterthur Portfolio* 24 (Spring 1989): 43–68.

INDEX

The names of the three architects who are the foci of this essay occur on nearly every page; they are not included in this index.

Hampden County Courthouse (Mass.),
21–22, fig. 11
Harrison, Benjamin, 1
Hartford, Conn.: Cheney building, 47
Hastings, Thomas, 32
Haviland, John, 17
Hay, John, house (Washington, D.C.),
54
Hayden building (Boston), 47, fig. 27
Henderson, F. B., house (Elmhurst,
Ill.), 133
*Henry Hobson Richardson and His
Works* (Van Rensselaer), 6, 82
Heurtley, Arthur, house (Oak Park,
Ill.), 130–32, figs. 85, 86
Hewitt, George M., 16, 71–72, figs. 6,
48
Hickox, Warren, house (Kankakee,
Ill.), 137
Higginson, F. L., house (Boston), 54
Highland Park, Ill., Ward Willits
house, xix, 134–35, 140, figs. 89, 90
High School (Worcester, Mass.), 20
Hillside Home School (Spring Green,
Wis.), 150
Hinsdale, Ill.: Frederick Bagley house,
119, 127
"Hints to Designers" (Furness), 74
Historicism, 13
Hobbs, Isaac H., 138
Hobbs's Architecture (Hobbs), 138
Holabird and Roche, 93
"Home in a Prairie Town" (Wright),
133, figs. 87, 88
Homes for the People (Wheeler), 138
Ho-o-den (Columbian Exposition, Chi-
cago), 137
Hooper, E. W., 35
Hospice in the Alps project (Guadet),
10, 25, 38, fig. 2
Hospital project (Richardson), 19–20
House Beautiful (Gannett), 142, figs.
94, 95
Houses of Parliament (London), 30,
85
Hull-House (Chicago), 141
Hunt, Richard Morris, 9, 12, 14, 17,
64–66, fig. 44
Husser, Joseph W., house (Chicago),
125–26, 133, fig. 81

"I and My Chimney" (Melville), 139
"Illinois" skyscraper project (Wright),
146
Inland Architect, 117
Interstate Architect and Builder, 4
"In the Cause of Architecture"
(Wright), 136, 137, 146

Jackson house, 138
Jayne building (Philadelphia), 76
Jefferson, Thomas, 58, 138, 150, 152
Jeffersonian, 7, 148
Jefferson Market Courthouse (New
York), 14, figs. 4, 30
Jenney, William Le Baron, 70, 102
Johnson Wax Company Research
Tower (Racine, Wis.), 146
Johnston, William, 76
Jones, Owen, 72, 74, 107, 142

Kahn, Louis I., 10
Kankakee, Ill.: B. Harley Bradley
house, 133, 137; Warren Hickox
house, 137
Kaplan, Justin, 80
Kehilath Anshe Ma'ariv Synagogue
(Chicago), 89, 111, fig. 58
"Kindergarten Chats" (Sullivan), 4–5,
83
King's College Chapel (Cambridge), 13
Knisely factory (Chicago), 79
Kohn, Fanny, house (Chicago), 80, fig.
53

Labrouste, Théodore, 9
Ladies' Home Journal, 133, 140, 148
LaGrange, Ill.: Cooper house barn proj-
ect (Wright), 126
Lake Monona Boat House project
(Wright), 126
Lake or River Villa project (Downing),
152, fig. 92
"Lamp of Sacrifice" (Ruskin), 41
Langwater (F. L. Ames estate, North
Easton, Mass.), 38, 59
Larkin Company Administration build-
ing (Buffalo), 116, 126, 137
Law Courts (London), 23
Leaves of Grass (Whitman), 80, 114
Ledoux, Claude-Nicolas, 119